T0197119

20 MINUTE PHONEMIC TRAINING FOR DYSLEXIA, AUDITORY PROCESSING, AND SPELLING

CVC, CCV, CCVC, CVCC, CCVCC Sets

Small Group and Individual Lessons For:
Phonemic Tasks for: Blending-Segmenting-Deletion-Isolation
Short Vowel Discrimination
Auditory Memory
Auditory Tracking, Phoneme Sequencing

CVC, CCV, CCVC, CVCC, CCVCC Reading Exercises
At Word and Sentence Levels

CVC, CCV, CCVC, CVCC, CCVCC Spelling Exercises
At Word and Sentence Levels

Alphabetic Principle
with Phonic Rule Chart and Word Lists for Phonic Spelling Rules

Included Are:

Reproducible Exercise Sheets, Record Form, Sample Goals &
Objectives for Interventions or Individual Education Plans
[IEP], Informal Assessment, Glossary of Terms
Organized by oral motor placement of sounds

Vickie Dinsmore, Speech Language Pathologist, M.Ed.
Copyright 2017

20 MINUTE PHONEMIC TRAINING FOR DYSLEXIA, AUDITORY PROCESSING, AND SPELLING

A Complete Resource for Speech Pathologists, Intervention Specialists, and Reading Tutors

Vickie Dinsmore

Speech Language Pathologist, M.Ed.

20 Minute Phonemic Training for Dyslexia, Auditory Processing, and Spelling
A Complete Resource for Speech Pathologists, Intervention Specialists, and Reading Tutors

iUniverse books may be ordered through booksellers or by contacting:

iUniverse
1663 Liberty Drive
Bloomington, IN 47403
www.iuniverse.com
1-800-Authors (1-800-288-4677)

Because of the dynamic nature of the Internet, any web addresses or links contained in this book may have changed since publication and may no longer be valid. The views expressed in this work are solely those of the author and do not necessarily reflect the views of the publisher, and the publisher hereby disclaims any responsibility for them.

Any people depicted in stock imagery provided by Thinkstock are models,
and such images are being used for illustrative purposes only.
Certain stock imagery © Thinkstock.

ISBN: 978-1-5320-2879-3 (sc)
ISBN: 978-1-5320-2878-6 (e)

Print information available on the last page.

iUniverse rev. date: 11/13/2017

CONTENTS

CVC SET 1
SHORT VOWEL TONES

CVC SET 2
LONG AND SHORT VOWEL TONES

CCV and CCVC SET 3
LONG AND SHORT VOWEL TONES

INTRODUCTION

20 Minute Phonemic Training for Dyslexia, Auditory Processing, and Spelling provides speech language pathologists and intervention specialists with strategies and a systematic process to address phonemic skill developmental delays that result in reading and writing fluency delays and disorders. The exercises featured support Reading and Writing skill development in the classroom by first developing skills in a small group or individual setting. The system presented develops phonemic and phonological awareness, auditory memory for sounds in words, auditory discrimination between phonemes and mapping of phonemes to letters.

For some students, classroom lessons about rhyme, learning to identify beginning, middle and ending sounds in words and learning word families and phonic rule patterns are not enough to enable them to understand how sounds and letters work together to form the written word. Their auditory systems prevent them from "making sense" of the sound system of our language. {See notes at the end of this section}

The exercises in *20 Minute Phonemic Training for Dyslexia, Auditory Processing, and Spelling* provide 'motor' clues/cues to help students match what they 'feel 'with what they hear and see. Providing one sensory [motor or "feeling"] cue between each syllable enables students to make sense of sound/letter relationships and phonic rules governing the English language.

Only ONE sound changes between each syllable to simplify the task of finding sound changes between words. Real words are used for MOST phoneme changes. Learning to recognize when a word is not a word also helps students realize when something does not make sense to cue them to reread for comprehension. Each vowel tone presents as a comparison between only two vowel tones at a time. Combinations of tones are paired by similarity in tone and proximity of production in the mouth. Words presented in similar pairs support development of auditory discrimination between vowel tones, voiced to voiceless phonemes, and other similar phonemes.

In the glossary, a list of labels is included for the descriptive labels used to group sounds by the movements of tongue, jaw, and lips along with meanings of words from the lists that may be unfamiliar to typical children.

A phonic rule chart is included to identify sound and letter patterns associated with short and long vowels {Appendix D}. Some pages contain spellings for phonic rule patterns. The phonic chart shows how vowel sounds determine spelling patterns.

Endnotes:

Dr. Martha Burns reviewed medical research of brain imaging as related to speech, language, auditory, and reading development over the past recent years. She presented summaries of the evidence with conclusions relating to therapy. See related locations for her presentations in:

Burns, Martha, Ph.D. "Auditory Processing Disorders, Dyslexia and Apraxia: Assessments and Evidence-Based Interventions- Review of Neuroscience Applications and APD" https://www.northernspeech.com/language-communication-disorders/auditory-processing-disorders-dyslexia-and-apraxia-assessments-and-evidence-based-interventions/

Burns, Martha Ph.D. "Training Auditory Processing in Children with Autism Spectrum Disorders and other Developmental Disabilities,"https://www.northernspeech.com/uploads/images/e05/e05-Handout-PDF.pdf

Martha S. Burns, Ph.D. Director of Neuroscience Education Scientific Learning Corporation Adjunct Associate Professor Northwestern University February 28, 2015, "Update on Neuroscience Applications to Treating Speech, Language and Cognitive Disorders", http://www.scilearn.com/sites/default/files/pdf/presentations vc/burns - feb 28th morning session - final 0.pdf

Dr. Kenn, Apel has researched spelling skills and neural development as relates to reading and written language development for many years. See related locations for some of his research in:

Kenn, Apel*,1, Julie J. Masterson2 "Comparing the Spelling and Reading Abilities of Students With Cochlear Implants and Students With Typical Hearing"; Journal of Deaf Studies and Deaf Education, 2015, 125–135; doi:10.1093/deafed/env002 Advance Access publication February 17, 2015 Empirical Manuscript

Kenn, Apel and Julie J. Masterson featured Language Speech and Hearing Services in the Schools July 2001, Vol. 32, 182-195. doi:10.1044/0161-1461(2001/017)

Find additional researchers and their work listed in the Bibliography.

BEFORE BEGINNING

A review of standardized assessment information from tests like the "Phonological Awareness Test from Linguisystems, Inc. 2007" is recommended. "The Phonological Awareness Test" results will indicate how the student blends tones for decoding purposes when sounding out words. A word level spelling sample assessment is included in the next section to aid the clinician in the selection of appropriate lists provided in *20 Minute Phonemic Training for Dyslexia, Auditory Processing, and Spelling.* In addition, a review of reading, writing and spelling samples from the classroom is recommended prior to diagnosis and selection of materials for implementation in the therapy setting. Analysis of the assessment results will reveal specific vowel tones and consonant combinations the student consistently misses when spelling and writing words.

Classroom teachers today have many instructional strategies for developing phonemic awareness at their disposal in pre-school, kindergarten and the primary grades. When students struggle, they provide individualized interventions, or learning activities, to support each student's needs. However, in many situations, the classroom teacher may not possess the level of training in oral motor skills, speech sound articulation, or auditory discrimination skill development and/or they simply may not have adequate time available for intensive, individualized instruction for the intense needs of a student demonstrating severe delay or disorder in this area. The data collected by the classroom teacher during the intervention process is also a rich resource for the Intervention Specialist, Reading Specialist, or Speech Language Pathologist to use.

The typical student, who will benefit most, is reading six months to two years below grade level, writing very little and what they write is not decodable due to poor spelling. Math calculations are often an area of strength. This student will likely have a history of language and/or articulation delay impairment often accompanied with a history of middle ear infection with or without mild, intermittent hearing loss.

As with learning any skill {i.e. playing an instrument, shooting hoops or riding a bike}, listening, remembering and learning sounds, letter recognition and their relationship to sounds, reading and writing requires adequate exposure through time and practice. Kindly allow yourself and your student adequate instructional frequency and time to develop skills. A minimum of two thirty minute sessions per week is recommended. Three sessions weekly is optimal. The actual lesson requires twenty minutes for most students. Thirty minutes allows five minutes for transition into the lesson and another five minutes transition for sharing a summary of feedback to the student at the end of the lesson. Summary feedback is important for student motivation.

PHONEMIC ASSESSMENT

Read the first list of words found in Appendix A to the student as a teacher might for a spelling test. If the student spells seventy percent or more of the words correctly, give them the second list.

Phonemic Sets One and Two apply for students failing to achieve at least 80% accuracy on the first list.

Phonemic Sets Three and Four apply for students failing to achieve at least eighty percent accuracy on the second list.

The first list samples ability to map sounds to letters and discriminate between voiced and voiceless phonemes [p/b; t/d; s/z; f/th], short vowel tones and long vowel tones, and apply the 'final e' rule to a long vowel.

The second list samples ability to discriminate and represent all sounds in blends when writing, and apply short vowel phonic rule spelling patterns in one-syllable words.

The third list samples ability to apply consonant doubling and –le syllables in two syllable words.

If students can write the phonemes correctly, they are usually able to hear the sound differences. Ability to apply phonic rules for long and short vowel tones such as 'final e' rule, floss rule, or –ck rule may also be analyzed from the samples taken. Grids showing the types of sounds and their combinations are included in Appendix A to guide in the selection of practice pages.

Additional resources for the oral motor placement of the jaw, lips, and tongue are located in Appendix B. Students often benefit from seeing the location of the jaw and shape of the lips in relationship to the tone of vowel sounds. Photos of lips with jaw placement are also included for each vowel tone.

DIRECTIONS FOR 20 MINUTE PHONEMICS

Ten sound combinations are included in each session. Individual sessions are ideal, but two students with similar needs work well together also. Sessions should be thirty minutes in duration to allow for response to errors initially spaced two to three times per week for maximum growth and reduced overall length of therapy. Yes, the word therapy applies because students are training and developing the brain to discriminate between sound differences while creating synaptic connections and neural pathways between motor, auditory, visual and lexical nodes of the brain. {See Bibliography – Burns, Martha}

The assessment word lists will guide selection of the exercises targeting the specific sound combinations the child needs, while the Phonological Awareness Test will guide selection of the exercises targeting the specific skills needing development. The recording page allows space for recording blending, segmenting, auditory tracking, reading, spelling the words, and spelling words in dictated sentences. Only complete those skill tasks needed by the student. For example, many students are capable of blending, but cannot segment or may track sounds well, but are unable to blend. In those instances, use the stronger skill to guide development of the weaker skill, but once the student begins to demonstrate the weaker skill to seventy percent accuracy, remove the strength skill from lessons. You may record "NA" [Not Applicable] in those spaces of the recording sheet.

Give assessments and complete your analysis as described in the previous section. After you analyze the errors and error patterns to determine, which sounds or combinations of sounds need remediation. select the exercise lists matching those sounds or sound patterns. For example, you will find many students cannot discriminate between the short vowel tones and/or long vowel tones. In those cases, select CVC List 1. If the student is able to discriminate between most short vowel tones, but struggles with /b/ and /d/ and the vowel tones for short /a/ and /e/, then select lists Five, Fifteen and Twenty-Five to begin. Others will struggle with voiced and voiceless consonants. Still others will not hear the differences between consonant digraphs. Some will struggle with all of the tasks. You will also find students who have the notion that the letter name is the letter sound. Select lists that compare the errored sound combinations the student is making.

When students need to develop phoneme to letter associations for short vowel tones, begin with the CVC short vowel section. This section presents short vowel tones in a hierarchy from widest disparity in jaw position moving to closest proximity in jaw position. Presenting the tones in this manner enables the student to engage motor feedback for establishing stable tone recognition, production recognition of each tone and correct mapping to letters. You may find these same students do not like to sing and cannot sing a melody on key. Singing tones to blend them, as a model and as an exercise, is a useful strategy at this skill level. Modify familiar tunes like "Twinkle, Twinkle Little Star" or "Row Row Row Your Boat."

Another strategy for short vowel tone recognition is the mnemonic sentence "Is Eddy At Uncle Ollie's." The first sound in each word is a short vowel tone. The tones present from jaw closed with tongue high to jaw open with tongue low.

Is Eddy at Uncle Ollie's?

AFTER THE PAGES ARE SELECTED

Step One. Begin by speaking each of the sounds within the first word on the list one sound at a time [you area segmenting]. Ask the student to tell you the word [the student is blending the phonemes]. Nearly all are real words, but may be unknown to the student. Talk about word meanings when this arises. Occasionally nonsense words are included. When a list contains a nonsense word, I challenge them to find the nonsense word in today's list. Use this as an opportunity to teach recognition of errors in decoding or spelling by noting that a word does not make sense.

Step Two: Give the student the circle & triangle page with something to use for marking the circles [stickers, ink stamper, marker OR paint dauber]. Say each syllable and ask the student to repeat the word, while saying each sound [segmenting] in the word and marking a shape for each sound {phoneme} in the syllable. {Hint: Paint Daubers are the fastest tool}. For each syllable after the first one, they will only mark a circle for the 'different' phoneme from the PREVIOUS word. This exercise requires them to segment, remember, sequence and compare the sounds in both syllables. At first, they will have trouble doing this. Model the activity by pointing to each shape and segmenting the sounds in chorus with the student. Then ask questions for each sound comparison to help them learn how to compare the sounds.

For example using the words "pit & pet" - prompt "Tell me the sounds in pit." "Tell me the sounds in pet." Which sound is different in the second word?

If they cannot find the different sound, say, "Tell me the first sound in pit and the first sound in pet." "Are the sounds the same or different? " "What do you feel when you say ____ ["p"] sound?" "Which word does /i/ [or /e/] go with in our sentence – Is Eddy At Uncle Ollie's?" Say "/i/ - **is** or /i/ **Eddy**." Do this for each phoneme in the sequence until they arrive at the correct sound change.

Sometimes they will not get it. When this occurs, model with a mirror and repeat the two sounds while explaining the difference in movement. Use questions like, "What part of your mouth is moving?" or "Does your jaw go up or down when you say /i/ then /e/?"

Continue through the list until all 10 syllables are completed.

Removing one sound from some words forms a new word. This is called 'deletion'. Deletion tally spaces are included on the record page for those items. At CVC level this is not a significant activity, however it is a valuable skill when learning to segment and spell words containing initial and final blends. For example, when one sound is removed the following words may be created: pat/at; slip/lip; slip/sip, etc.

A separate page is included at the beginning of Set 3 for practicing sound reversals. Sound reversals often present in student writing when students have trouble sequencing sounds. Teaching them deliberate sound reversing is helpful when addressing sequencing issues. For example, pit/tip, tap/pat; bat/tab; flit/felt; or trim/term.

Step Three. Using the list and sentence pages, ask them to read the words they just blended, segmented and 'painted' {auditory tracking}. When students are consistently successful with any of the individual skills, skip those exercises. Note: some sight words are included in the sentences. Sight words are normally part of the classroom reading instruction and are important in the development of reading, although not useful as the ONLY tool in the development of reading and writing skills.

Step Four. Finally, read the syllables for the student to write, [like a spelling test]. When writing, have them use the sentence "Is Eddy At Uncle Ollie's" for comparing the vowel tones to letters to aid correct mapping of short vowel tones to letters. [I post the picture of Eddy at his Uncle Ollie's home on a wall nearby as a reminder to the student to use the mnemonic tool for discrimination between short vowel tones.] {Information about how to get color poster copies of the "Eddy" picture, and the Phonic chart in Appendix D is available at www.20MinutePhonemicTraining. com. Write the percentage of correctly blended, segmented, tracked, read, and written syllables on the teacher record page. Write "NA" if the student does not need to practice a task

When proficient in the use of mouthing and segmenting sounds as they write and spell words on the lists to eighty percent accuracy, give them the dictated sentence from the "sentence reading list" for the word set the student is studying. Students respond well to immediate feedback when writing words and sentences, so give them a score for each list and each sentence immediately. For example, you may write "4 of 7" and underline the correctly spelled words immediately after writing a dictated sentence.

Periodically, it is helpful to tell the students a story and ask them to rewrite it in their own words. I find they love to hear stories about animals, their teacher's childhood, or plans for upcoming events in the school. This eliminates the need for them to generate a story, yet requires them to generate sentences. As with dictated sentences, provide immediate feedback regarding the number of words correctly spelled. They also enjoy keeping a graph using colored pencils to track their own progress over time. While on the topic of color most children, who are resistant to writing, love to write with colored gel pens. Therefore, I keep a cup filled with an assortment of colors on the table at all times.

STRATEGIES FOR BLENDING WHEN STUDENTS STRUGGLE

1. Model: Use marbles that are flat on one side. Slide them together as you connect the sounds. Use the phrase 'voice on' or 'sing' the sounds. Give student marbles to repeat.
2. Model: Place paper squares of different shapes or colors before the student. Leave spaces between each paper. Touch each paper as you speak each sound [segmented] in the word, then push the papers together and speak the syllable with sounds blended. Allow student to 'blend' [push together] the papers with the sounds.
3. Model: Make a dot for each sound on a paper. Then use a crayon and with 'voice on', draw a flowing line as you connect the sounds. Give student crayon and paper to repeat.
4. Model: Stroke your arm, voice on, as you connect the sounds. Ask them to repeat.
5. Place paper shapes on the floor in a sequence [for example: circle, triangle, square = pat; or circle, triangle, circle = pop] and step on each one while speaking a phoneme for a word. Next, ask the student to repeat the sequence / movement and then sing or say the word

STRATEGIES FOR TRACKING AND SEGMENTING SOUND CHANGES BETWEEN SYLLABLES

1. Say the syllable aloud first. Talk about movement. Every mouth movement creates a new sound. Practice with letter names. The letter B or b name is two movements and two sounds /b/ +/e/. Many of the consonant letter names contain their sound, but also have another sound connected to them. B,D,J,K,P,Q,T,V,Z all have their sound at the beginning of their names. F,L,M,N,R,S,X. and C [has two sounds – see the phonic table in the Appendix D]. G,H,W,Y say sounds that are different from their letter names.
2. Next, touch each shape as you speak each sound. Stop your voice between sounds.
3. If the student cannot remember the previous syllable for comparison:
   Touch the next row of shapes and say the new word.
   Touch the previous row and repeat that word.
   Have the student repeat both words and touch/speak the sounds in each word to compare the two and find the 'change' in the second word.
4. Cue them to compare each jaw or tongue movement between words.
5. Be ready to say the sound with the student until they are able to remember and segment on their own.
6. Tell them: Listen to yourself and think about how your mouth, tongue and lips are moving for each sound. Think about how your mouth, tongue and lips are moving in the second word.

READING

The reading exercise is the application of skills practiced. The previous exercises address the common core objectives for phonological and phonemic awareness. Awareness and ability to manipulate sounds in words is foundational to decoding.

When students are decoding unknown words, remind them to think about matching sounds with letters.

Say:_"Be sure to blend the sounds. Keep your voice turned on." If difficulties persist, have them begin with the last sound and add one sound at a time until all sounds are blended; this is sometimes called 'backward chaining.'

Another strategy is to speak the initial and final blends as units and 'sing' the sounds together, until they reach automaticity with the mapping and blending of phonemes to letters.

In addition to reading the sentences provided, the student should be reading short fluency passages containing primarily sight words at the kindergarten and first grade level with CVC words for those students working with Set 1. Such passages are available for all syllable levels on Teachers Pay Teachers on the "Kindergarten Connection" store page. Reading A-Z also has leveled fluency passages. I find a break from the exercises to repeatedly read a passage three times in a row for one minute each time, is a tangible demonstration to the student of their own progress and highly motivational. Having the student chart, the number of words read and the number of errors made within a minute and repeatedly reading a passage provides them with visual proof of their learning progress.

WRITING

Writing and spelling require ability to recognize phonemes and map them to letters when writing. The writing exercise is the application of skills practiced. Some useful strategies include:

Remind them to say each sound in the syllable as they write it.

Tell them: Match the sounds to the letters. Use your mouth movements to help you match the sounds and letters.

Give them water and a paintbrush and ask them to say each sound while painting the corresponding letters or letter combinations to spell words.

Practice skywriting. Model the spelling by writing it with your finger in the air and ask them to tell you the sequence of letters used by stating each sound rather than the letter names. This may become a blending task as well if only phonemes are presented and they must blend the phonemes as well as identify and map the letters to sounds. This exercise helps to develop visual with auditory memory while using large muscle movement. Writing on the tabletop with fingers is another variation on this activity. One note of caution: Be sure the student 'sees' the movement [letters] from left to right. If you are sitting across from the student, you will need to write backwards from right to left!

At this time, I would like to take a moment to say a few words about the letters 'b' and 'd'. Many teachers and parents believe that the reversal of 'b' and 'd' when writing is a symptom of dyslexia. I would disagree. I find that it is more a symptom of the overall confusion some children encounter when attempting to develop phonemic mapping and processing skills. Trying to make sense of which sounds go with which letters AND how many sounds are in a word AND remembering how and when to write capital and lower case letters AND how to punctuate AND phonic rules for spelling different sound combinations... AND..you get the idea. Somehow mixing up 'b' and' 'd' seems rather normal!

To help your student, emphasize that the sound /b/ begins with the lips together, the letter is written with the line first [represents lips together], and the 'air bump' comes after the line in a left to right progression. Model writing the letter while you explain and speak the sound. Likewise, tell them if they do not feel their lips come together when speaking the /d/ sound, then the 'air bump' comes first and the line second in a left to right progression. They will soon stop reversing /b/ and /d/ when writing. For this strategy to work, it is imperative that they speak the sounds in the words as they are writing them, at least sub-vocally with mouth movement.

DAY 1 WITH THE STUDENT: THE SOUND AND LETTER STORY

The following story helps children to understand the sound to words and letters connection.

"You learned to talk all by yourself. You connected many sounds to say many words when you were very little. Words are made of lots of sounds that are connected together."

At this point, I begin to make each sound in their name while reaching out into the air as if grasping it and setting it into position from their left to right before their face. "[/t/ - /o/ - /m/ /ee/].

"There. Could you see those sounds? Can you see your name up there? Of course not! We cannot see sounds! But sounds are all around us. We just cannot see them. We hear them. I imagine that a very long time ago, when the first people were learning to talk to each other, they had a problem. They did not have cars, radio, or telephones. When they wanted to tell you something, they had to SEE you. They could not even mail a letter! They also did NOT have books or letters to write words! So, they drew pictures, but they did not have paper either. They drew on the walls of their homes, in the dirt, or on rocks. They drew pictures of people, trees, and animals. They had one BIG problem. Some words they used could not be drawn, because they could not be seen'. If they wanted to tell you that something was 'easy' to do, they could not draw a picture of 'easy'. Then someone figured out that there are sounds inside each word -- /ee/-/z/ - /ee/. They made up 'pictures' for each /sound/ used in words, and letters were born. In our language there are really only forty four of these sounds, but we can make thousands of words by mixing up and adding sounds together to make lots of words."

"Letters are pictures of sounds. Now all they had to do was draw the 'picture, or letter' for each sound in a word and then someone else could look at the sound pictures, connect them together and say the word. Time passed. People were scattered all over the world. People started making rules about how to draw the sound pictures and which letters could sit next to other letters and different ways to spell words. That is how reading and writing words began."

Together, we are going to play with sounds and match them to the 'pictures'. We are going to be taking the sounds apart and putting them together until it is easy for you to read and write words.

See Appendix C for Student Forms and Record Forms

CVC SET 1

SHORT VOWEL TONES

CVC LABIALS, ALVOELARS, VOICED AND VOICELESS PAIRS

p, b, t, d, m, n, s, l, w

List One: p, b, d, d, m with short a and o:
tab, tap, dap, map, mop, mod, mad, bad, bod, bot

List Two: p, b, t, d, m, w with short a and i and includes irregular spelling with 'tt':
bam, bad, bid, did, dip, whip, whap, map, mat, mitt

List Three: p, b, t, d, m, n with short e and i:
pip, pep, pet, bet, bed, bid, bin, Ben, bet, met

List Four: p, b, t, d, m with short a and u:
tum, tub, dub, pub, pup, Pap, pat, putt, but, bat

List Five : p, b, t, d, m with short a and e:
map, mat, met, med mad, bad, bed, bet, pet, pat

List Six: p, b, t, d, m, n with short u and i:
mud, dud, bud, bid, bit, but, mutt, mitt, pit, pin

List Seven: b, t, d, n, m, s with short u and e -- *FLOSS rule [see phonic chart]*:
set, met, Mel, mull, dull, dell, bell, bet, but, nut

List Eight: p, b, d, m, n with short e and o:
pep, pen, pawn, pod, nod, Ned, med, mod, mop, bop

List Nine: b, t, m, n with short o and u and introduces the concept of silent 'b':
top, tot, Tom, tum, numb, bum, bomb, bot, not, nut

List Ten: b, t, d, l, m with short o and i and includes the concept of silent 'b':
dip, tip, top, bop, lop, lip, limb, Tim, Tom, mom

CVC LABIALS, ALVOELARS, VOICED AND VOICELESS PAIRS

p, b, t, d, m, n, s, l, w

Lists One through Ten Reading Page

List One:
tab, tap, dap, map, mop, mod, mad, bad, bod, bot

List Two:
bam, bad, bid, did, dip, whip, whap, map, mat, mitt

List Three:
pip, pep, pet, bet, bed, bid, bin, Ben, bet, met

List Four:
tum, tub, dub, pub, pup, Pap, pat, putt, but, bat

List Five:
map, mat, met, med mad, bad, bed, bet, pet pat

List Six:
mud, dud, bud, bid, bit, but, mutt, mitt, pit, pin

List Seven:
set, met, Mel, mull, dull, dell, bell, bet, but, nut

List Eight:
pep, pen, pawn, pod, nod, Ned, med, mod, mop, bop

List Nine:
top, tot, Tom, tum, numb, bum, bomb, bot, not, nut

List Ten:
dip, tip, top, bop, lop, lip, limb, Tim, Tom, mom

CVC LABIALS, ALVOELARS, VOICED AND VOICELESS PAIRS

p, b, t, d, m, n, s, l, w

Sentences for Reading and Dictation
for lists One through Ten

1. Tom had a pit and bit his lip.

2. Ross was boss of the bus and the jet.

3. Dip the tip of the limb in the well.

4. Mom put a dull pin in the map.

5. Ned bet a bat set on Ben to win.

6. Tom put a nut, a bat, and a pen on the mat.

7. Dad has a pen, and a pawn, but not a nut.

8. Mel put the nut in the mud.

9. Tim met Ned by the net with Bud.

10. Set the mitt and the tab on top of the bed.

CVC LABIALS, ALVEOLAR, PALATALS, DENTALS VOICED AND VOICELESS PAIRS

p, b, m, n, f, v, l, r, t, d, ch, sh, s, th, j, g, w

List Eleven: b, j, r, with short a and o –*tch phonic rule for short vowels*:
botch, batch, bam, jam, jab, job, lob, rob, Bob, Bab

List Twelve: p, b, t, m, w, s, sh, th with short a and i -- *FLOSS rule & 'y' for short 'i'*:
wish, wit, with, pith, path, bath, bass, mass, miss, myth

List Thirteen: b, t, d, w, f, n, l and t, m, l, s, sh, ch, j with short e and i -- *FLOSS, -tch 2 sounds of 'g'*:
nib, fib, fit, wit, lit, let, wet, wed, fed, Feb
mess, mesh, met, mitt, Mitch, miss, mill, Jill, gel, jet

List Fourteen: p, b, m, n, f, l,ch, j with short a and u –*dge rule,-tch and FLOSS*:
fuzz, fudge, judge, nudge, budge, badge, batch, patch, latch, match

List Fifteen: p, m, n, w, v, s, ch, j with short a and e -- *FLOSS rule and the second sound of 'g' [see phonic rule chart]*:
Pam, jam, gem, Jess, chess, Wes, when, men, man, van

List Sixteen: m, l, f, s, z, th, ch with short u and i –*FLOSS rule*:
sis, this, thus, muss, fuss, fuzz, fizz, fill, chill, mill

List Seventeen: b, t, d, v, n, r, with short u and e: –*dge and silent w*:
nut, net, vet, bet, but, budge, bud, bed, red, wren

List Eighteen: m, l, f, s, ch, j with short e and o—*includes the FLOSS rule*:
fess, less, loss, moss, mess, chess, Chet, jet, jot, lot

List Nineteen: b, t, n, r, s with short o and u- *includes FLOSS rule and one deviation*:
not, rot, rut, rub, rob, Ross, boss, bus, but, bot

List Twenty: b, t, m, f, l, s, z, sh, r with short o and i- *includes FLOSS rule*:
miss, moss, Ross, boss, loss, lot, lit, fit, fizz, fish

*two lists are included due to frequent intense need for discrimination between short e and i phonemes

CVC LABIALS, ALVEOLAR, PALATALS, DENTALS VOICED AND VOICELESS PAIRS

Lists Eleven through Twenty Reading Page

List Eleven:
botch, batch, bam, jam, jab, job, lob, rob, Bob, Bab

List Twelve:
wish, wit, with, pith, path, bath, bass, mass, miss, myth

List Thirteen:
nib, fib, fit, wit, lit, let, wet, wed, fed, Feb
mess, mesh, met, mitt, Mitch, miss, mill, Jill, gel, jet

List Fourteen:
fuzz, fudge, judge, nudge, budge, badge, batch, patch, latch, match

List Fifteen:
Pam, jam, gem, Jess, chess, Wes, when, men, man, van

List Sixteen:
sis, this, thus, muss, fuss, fuzz, fizz, fill, chill, mill

List Seventeen:
nut, net, vet, bet, but, budge, bud, bed, red, wren

List Eighteen:
fess, less, loss, moss, mess, chess, Chet, jet, jot, lot

List Nineteen:
not, rot, rut, rub, rob, Ross, boss, bus, but, bot

List Twenty:
miss, moss, Ross, boss, loss, lot, lit, fit, fizz, fish

CVC LABIALS, ALVEOLAR, PALATALS, DENTALS VOICED AND VOICELESS PAIRS

p, b, m, n, f, l, r, t, d, ch, sh, s, th, j, g, w

Sentences for Reading and Dictation
for lists Eleven through Twenty

1. Jess let Chet check the chess set.

2. Ross was boss of the bus and the jet.

3. This fish will not budge to miss the moss.

4. The mess is less on the lot.

5. Patch the latch then match the fudge.

6. Fill and chill the cup with fizz and fuzz.

7. Mitch will miss Jill at the mill.

8. Bob will jam the batch of fudge in the jet.

9. I wish Bab did not fuss with Chet.

10. The vet bet his check on the pet.

CVC VELARS, ALVEOLAR, PALATALS

k, g, t, d, n, l, sh, ch, j, r,

List Twenty-One: t, d, g, k [c] with short a and o:
cot, cod, cad, tad, tag, tog, Todd, God, got, dot

List Twenty-Two: t, r, k [c], g, sh with short a and i –*ck phonic rule and silent w*:
gal, gad, rad, rack, Rick, rid, writ, rat, cat, cash

List Twenty Three: t, d, l, r, k, g, j with short e and i: –*ck, FLOSS, two sounds g*:
deck, dell, tell, gel, Jill, jig, rig, rid, lid, lick

List Twenty-four: g, l, r, sh with short a and u:
lug, lag, gag, shag, rag, rug, rut, gut, gull, lull

List Twenty-Five: t, d, k, g, l, sh with short a and e -*ck rule* :
shed, shad, lad, led, let, leg, lag, shag, shack, knack

List Twenty-Six: t, l, r, k [c], g with short u and i- –*ck rule*:
cud, kid, rid, rig, rug, lug, luck, tuck, chuck, chick, tick

List Twenty-Seven: d, l, k, g, sh, ch with short u and e: -*ck and FLOSS*:
check, deck, duck, dull, gull, gush, rush, lush, lug, leg

List Twenty- Eight: t, d, l, k, g, ch with short e and o:-*ck and FLOSS*:
cog, keg, leg, log, dog, doll, tall, talk, chock, check

List Twenty-Nine: t, d, n, k [c],g, sh, j with short o and u:
nut, not, cot, shot, jot, jut, shut, gut, cut, cud

List Thirty: t, d, l, k, r with short o and i: –*ck rule* :
kick, kit, lit, lid, rid, rod, rock, Rick, lick, lock

CVC VELARS, ALVEOLAR, PALATALS

k, g, t, d, n, l, sh, ch, j, r,

Lists Twenty One through Thirty Reading Page

List Twenty-One:
cot, cod, cad, tad, tag, tog, Todd, God, got, dot

List Twenty-Two:
gal, gad, rad, rack, Rick, rid, writ, rat, cat, cash

List Twenty-Three:
deck, dell, tell, gel, Jill, jig, rig, rid, lid, lick

List Twenty-Four:
lug, lag, gag, shag, rag, rug, rut, gut, gull, lull

List Twenty-Five:
shed, shad, lad, led, let, leg, lag, shag, shack, knack

List Twenty-Six:
cud, kid, rid, rig, rug, lug, luck, tuck, chuck, chick, tick

List Twenty-Seven:
check, deck, duck, dull, gull, gush, rush, lush, lug, leg

List Twenty-Eight:
cog, keg, leg, log, dog, doll, tall, talk, chock, check

List Twenty-Nine:
nut, not, cot, shot, jot, jut, shut, gut, cut, cud

List Thirty:
kick, kit, lit, lid, rid, rod, rock, Rick, lick, lock

CVC VELARS, ALVEOLAR, PALATALS

k, g, t, d, n, l, sh, ch, j, r,

Sentences for Reading and Dictation for Lists Twenty-One through Thirty

1. Rick can rock into the lid to get rid of the rat.

2. A kid cannot gut a cod fish.

3. The dog had a keg with a cog on its neck.

4. The duck and the gull can rush to check the shed.

5. Chuck had a chick with a tick on it.

6. Put the shad in the shed and the cod in the shack.

7. Todd can lug a rat and a gull to the deck.

8. Jill put a lid and a deck on the rig.

9. The gal with Rick got rid of his cat and his cash.

10. The cot for the cod was a tad too much.

CVC SET 2

LONG
AND
SHORT
VOWEL
TONES

CVC LONG AND SHORT VOWELS WITH LABIALS, ALVEOLAR, VOICED AND VOICELESS PAIRS

p, b, m, n, f, l, r, t, d, ch, sh, s, th, j, g, w

List One: p, t, d, m, k with a and o - *introducing short o as [-al-] and final e:*
tape, tap, tack, take, talk, top, mop, mope, map, mad

List Two: p, b, d, n with a and i - *final e and [-ie-]* :
bid, bad, bade, bide, died, did, dip, din, Dane, dine

List Three: p, b, t, d, n, l with e and i - *final e, [-ee-], and [-ea-]:*
pipe, peep, Pete, beet, bet, bed, Ben, bean, lean, line

List Four: p, b, t, d, l, with a and u -- *final e and [-oo-]:*
tub, tube, lube, loop, dupe, poop, pup, Pap, pat, pate

List Five: b, t, d, m, with a and e --*final e, [-ee-]*
mate, meet, met, med, mad, made, bade, bad, bed, bet

List Six: b, t, d u and i - *final e, [-ie-], [oo]:*
dud, dude, died, did, bid, bide, bite, boot, but, bud

List Seven: t, d, m, l, s with u and e - *FLOSS, [-ea-], [ee]:*
seat, set, met, meet, mutt, mull, mule, Mel, meal, deal

List Eight: p, t, d, f, l with e and o - *final e, [-au-], [-ee-], [-ea-], -al-]:*
peep, peal, pole, Paul, tall, teal, tell, fell, fed, feed

List Nine: b, t, m, n with short o and u - *[-oo-] and final e:*
tote, toot, tot, Tom, tome, tone, tune, boon, bun, bum

List Ten: w, l, m, n with o and i - *final e, silent b and [y] for short i:*
Nome, dome, Dom, dim, dime, lime, limb, Lynn, line, wine

CVC LONG AND SHORT VOWELS WITH LABIALS, ALVEOLAR, VOICED AND VOICELESS PAIRS

p, b, m, n, f, l, r, t, d, ch, sh, s, th, j, g, w

Lists One through Ten Reading Page

List One:
tape, tap, tack, take, talk, top, mop, mope, map, mad

List Two:
bid, bad, bade, bide, died, did, dip, din, Dane, dine

List Three:
pipe, peep, Pete, beet, bet, bed, Ben, bean, lean, line

List Four:
tub, tube, lube, loop, dupe, poop, pup, Pap, pat, pate

List Five:
mate, meet, met, med, mad, made, bade, bad, bed, bet

List Six:
dud, dude, died, did, bid, bide, bite, boot, but, bud

List Seven;
seat, set, met, meet, mutt, mull, mule, Mel, meal, deal

List Eight:
peep, peal, pole, Paul, tall, teal, tell, fell, fed, feed

List Nine:
tote, toot, tot, Tom, tome, tone, tune, boon, bun, bum

List Ten:
Nome, dome, Dom, dim, dime, lime, limb, Lynn, line, wine

CVC LONG AND SHORT VOWELS WITH LABIALS, ALVEOLAR, VOICED AND VOICELESS PAIRS

p, b, t, d, m, n, s, l, w

Sentences for Reading and Dictation Lists One through Ten

1. Dan put tape on the mop that he made.

2. Dane will bide his time to dine with you.

3. Pete and Ben put a pipeline in the mine.

4. Pap put a loop of tube in the tub.

5. The shipmate Mel met made him mad.

6. The dude did bite his boot!

7. Mel sat in his seat to eat a meal with the mule.

8. Tell Paul that the tall pole fell.

9. At the toot of the tone the bun will be done.

10. Dom said, "Nope, I will not dip the dime in the lime."

CVC LABIALS, ALVEOLAR, PALATALS, DENTALS WITH LONG AND SHORT VOWELS

p, b, m, w, n, f, [ph], v, l, r, t, d, ch, sh, s, th, j, g,

List Eleven: b, t, d, l, m, n, r, sh, j with a and o:- *final e rule:*
tame, lame, shame, sham, Jan, ran, Ron, rob, robe, road

List Twelve: m, t, d, r with a and i: - *[-igh-], [-ai-], and [-ce-]:*
rid, rad, raid, race, rate, right, might, mate, mat

List Thirteen: t, m, l, s, ch, with e and i: *[-ce-], [-igh-], [-ea-], [-ee], and FLOSS:*
met, meet, might, mitt, Mitch, miss, mice, mess, less, lease

List Fourteen: t, m, z, f, v, j, with a and u – *[-oo-], [-ph-] and vowel effect on s and z:*
fuzz, fuse, phase, raise, rage, rave, rate, root, room

List Fifteen: p, m, n, v, r, j and t, n, l, sh, j *with a and e: two lists for extra practice—final e, [-ea,], [-ai,]; and final e [-ee-], -ea-], [-ai-], FLOSS**
them, jem, jam, Jan, van, vane, pane, rain, mane, mean,
sheen, teen, ten, Jen, jean, Jane, jail, shale, shall, shell

List Sixteen: l, m, f, s, z. sh, ch with u and i-*final e, [-oo-], FLOSS, and vowel effect on s and z:*
muss, muse, shoes, choose, fuse, fuss, fuzz, fizz, fill, file

List Seventeen: b, t, d, sh, ch, j with u and e: *[-oo-], [-ee-], -dge, [-ea-], -ch with long vowel:*
shoot, shut, sheet, beet, bet, but, budge, bud, bead, beach

List Eighteen: t, d, l, n, s, r with e and o:- *[-ee-], [-ea-], [-oa-], FLOSS, and vowel effect on s and z:*
leech, lead, led, load, toad, Todd, toss, Ross, rose, nose

List Nineteen: t, d, n, r with short o and u: - *silent w, final e [-oo-]:*
nut, not, note, wrote, rot, rut, root, rude, rode, rod

List Twenty: p, m, f, s, r with o and i: *[-igh-], [-ce], FLOSS, and vowel effect on s and z:*
fight, sight, sit, sis, miss, mice, rice, Ross, rose, pose

*two lists are included due to frequent intense need for discrimination between short e and i phonemes

CVC LABIALS, ALVEOLAR, PALATALS, DENTALS WITH LONG AND SHORT VOWELS

p, b, m, w, n, f, [ph], v, l, r, t, d, ch, sh, s, th, j, g,

Lists Eleven through Twenty Reading Page

List Eleven:
tame, lame, shame, sham, Jan, ran, Ron, rob, robe, road

List Twelve:
rid, rad, raid, race, rate, right, might, mate, mat

List Thirteen:
met, meet, might, mitt, Mitch, miss, mice, mess, less, lease

List Fourteen:
fuzz, fuse, phase, raise, rage, rave, rate, root, room

List Fifteen:
**them, jem, jam, Jan, van, vane, pane, rain, mane, mean
sheen, teen, ten, Jen, jean, Jane, jail, shale, shall, shell**

List Sixteen:
muss, muse, shoes, choose, fuse, fuss, fuzz, fizz, fill, file

List Seventeen:
shoot, shut, sheet, beet, bet, but, budge, bud, bead, beach

List Eighteen:
leech, lead, led, load, toad, Todd, toss, Ross, rose, nose

List Nineteen:
nut, not, note, wrote, rot, rut, root, rude, rode, rod

List Twenty:
fight, sight, sit, sis, miss, mice, rice, Ross, rose, pose

CVC LABIALS, ALVEOLAR, PALATALS, DENTALS WITH LONG AND SHORT VOWELS

p, b, m, w, n, f, [ph], v, l, r, t, d, ch, sh, s, th, j, g

Sentences for Reading and Dictation

1. Jan and Ron did put the tame roach in the race.

2. At this rate the mate might win the race.

3. Mitch might meet the mice that made the mess.

4. The root had room to raise the roof.

5. Jen and Jane drove the van in the rain.

6. If you choose those shoes, you might fuss with the fuzz on them.

7. The jail is shut and will not budge.

8. I choose the rose with a toad on it.

9. Ross rode a toad in the race with the leech.

10. Mitch and the mice will fight for the rice.

VELARS, ALVEOLAR, PALATALS, DENTALS WITH LONG AND SHORT VOWELS

k, g, t, d, n, l, sh, ch, j, r, th, f, v

List Twenty-One: t, d, f, k [c], l, r with a and o: -[-ough-], [-oa-], [-al-], [-ol-], *final e:*
cot, coat, code, cod, cough, call, kale, coal, roll, rode

List Twenty-Two: t, d, k [c], g, r, l with a and i:- *[-ai-], [-igh-], -ck, final e:*
gale, rail, rake, rack, Rick, rid, ride, right, kite, Kate

List Twenty-Three: d, n, l, s, ch, r with and i and e:- *[-ee-], [-ea-], silent w, -ck:*
deck, wreck, reek, seek, cheek, leak, lick, chick, check, neck

List Twenty-Four: m, t, l, s, sh, h, k [c], g, with a and u: *[-oo-], [-ui-], final e:*
hut, hat, hoot, shoot, suit, lute, late, Kate, cute, mute

List Twenty-Five: d, k, s, sh, ch with a and e: *[-ee-], [-ea-], -ck, final e, and long vowel with –ch:*
shack, shake, sake, sack, seek, seed, said, red, reed, reach

List Twenty-Six: t, d, k, g, with u and i: *-ck, and final e:*
tuck, tick, tike, like, lick, luck, Luke, Duke, duck, dug

List Twenty-Seven: t, d, l, f, j, r with u and e: *[-ue-], [-ea-], [-oo-], FLOSS, [-ew-] and final e:*
fell, fuel, jewel, duel, dell, dead, fed, red, rude, root

List Twenty-Eight: t, d, k, ch, r with e and o: *[-ee-], [-oa-], final e, -ck, silent w:*
Cheek, choke, check, deck, wreck, red, reed, rode, toad, code

List Twenty-Nine: t, n, k [c], sh, th, r, j with short o and u- *[-oa-], [-ough-], [-oo-], and final e:*
note, coat, cot, thought, shot, shoot, root, rot, jot, jute

List Thirty: p, t, d, l, k, r with o and i:- *[-igh-] and final e:*
kit, kite, light, lit, lid, rid, ride, rode, rope, ripe

VELARS, ALVEOLAR, PALATALS, DENTALS WITH LONG AND SHORT VOWELS

k, g, t, d, n, l, sh, ch, j, r, th, f, v

Lists Twenty One through Thirty Reading Page

List Twenty-One:
cot, coat, code, cod, cough, call, kale, coal, roll, rode

List Twenty-Two:
gale, rail, rake, rack, Rick, rid, right, kite, Kate, cat,

List Twenty-Three:
deck, wreck, reek, seek, cheek, leak, lick, chick, check, neck

List Twenty-Four:
hut, hat, hoot, shoot, suit, lute, late, Kate, cute, mute

List Twenty
shack, shake, sake, sack, seek, seed, said, red, reed, reach

List Twenty-Six:
tuck, tick, tike, like, lick, luck, Luke, Duke, duck, dug,

List Twenty-Seven:
fell, fuel, jewel, duel, dell, dead, fed, red, rude, root

List Twenty: Eight:
Cheek, choke, check, deck, wreck, red, reed, rode, toad

List Twenty-Nine:
note, coat, cot, thought, shot, shoot, root, rot, jot, jute

List Thirty:
kit, kite, light, lit, lid, rid, ride, rode, rope, ripe

VELARS, ALVEOLAR, PALATALS, DENTALS

k, g, t, d, n, l, sh, ch, j, r, th, f, v
with long and short vowels

Sentences for Reading and Dictation

1. He put the coat and the kale on the cot.

2. Rick got rid of the kite and the cat.

3. Check the chick on the deck with the leak.

4. Mute the TV in the hut for cute Kate the cat.

5. Reach in the shack and shake the sack.

6. Luke and Duke like to lick duck.

7. A dude in the dell was in a duel for a jewel.

8. The toad did choke on the reed by the hot deck.

9. Jot a note on the jute shoot.

10. Ride the kite that you made with the kit.

CCV AND CCVC SET 3

LONG
AND
SHORT
VOWEL
TONES

REVERSALS

The following list of two phoneme words is used to drill students in the order of motor and phoneme [sound]. Place two marbles of different colors or two small pieces of paper of different shapes before the student. Model the two sounds in different sequences to demonstrate how the order of sounds changes the word.

Please note: the following list is not a 'one sound change' chain of words. Therefore, the words are not intended for use with the student worksheets. However, the teacher record sheet includes space for recording student number of correct student responses. You may want to use tokens or game turns to count correct responses for reinforcement.

uth = the   zi = is
fo = off   chi = itch
sie = ice   li = ill
oyb =boy   ree = ear
eesh –=she   ni = in
oeg = go   knaw = on
ti = it   own = no
ieb = bye   eek = key
ees = see   koa = oak
eem = me   iet = tie
eat = tea   ire = rye
eeb = be   ied = dye
eep = pea   iep = pie
eef = fee   aed = day
vee = eve   aeth = they
lee = eel   air = ray
een = knee   ace = say
fi = if   ache = kay

/r/ Sound Sequence Instruction

The next three lists cover /r/ reversals. The /r/ sound is a vocalic phoneme that is difficult for many students to sequence. Cues to help include:

Ask the student to think about the position of the vowel tone in relationship to the first consonant.

1. "Does the /r/ sound come right after the first sound {free} or does it come right after the vowel sound {fear}?"
2. "Does the /r/ come right after the first sound {crud} or right before the last sound {curd}?

Tell them to "Think about how your mouth feels when you say the word as well as what you hear."

Practice segmenting the sound while touching manipulatives to help the student visualize the location of the /r/ phoneme in the sequence.

Practice Lists for /r/ phoneme reversals

List One CCV and VCC reversals for the /r/ sounds – or:
for, fro, bro, bore, poor, pro, throw, Thor, or, row

List Two One CCV and VCC reversals for the /r/ sounds – air and –ire:
air, rare, fair, fray, tray, tare, tire, try, fry, fire

List Three One CCV and VCC reversals for the /r/ sounds - ear and air:
fear, free, tree, tear, peer, pair, care, cray, crow, core

List Four CCVC and CVCC reversals:
breed, beard, feared, freed, creed, reed, road, crowed, cord, court

PRACTICE LISTS FOR /r/ PHONEME REVERSALS

Sentences for Reading and Dictation

1. A pro can throw a football to Thor.

2. Is it fair to set a tire on fire and smoke up the air?

3. I fear the three crows will tear up the pair of trees.

4. Poor bro, he cannot throw very far.

5. It is a rare person that can fray their jeans and not tear them.

6. Lend me your ear to hear the story of the free crow in the cray.

7. Plant your corn in a row, bro.

8. It was a fair fight for the friar, but he tore his coat on the tire.

9. Try not to fray the rare cloth.

10. Freedom is never free so we should take care of our freedom.

11. That breed of dog has a beard and should be feared when you see it on the road.

HOW TO TREAT SOUND REDUCTIONS AND REVERSALS

To help students recognize the presence of voiceless sounds and nasals, sometimes words with three sounds rather than four sounds are used when studying CCV, CCVC and CVCC syllables. Within each list, there is only one sound change between each word. Therefore, two stars may be marked to indicate a missing sound. For example, given the following CCVC exercise example:

When changing '**bride**' to '**bide,**' the /r/ is missing, so the second circle is marked.
Then when changing '**bide**' to '**bite**,' the /r/ is still missing, but the last sound also changed, so an **X** is placed in the second circle and the last space is marked.
When changing '**bite**' to '**bright**,' the /r/ returned, so the second circle is marked.

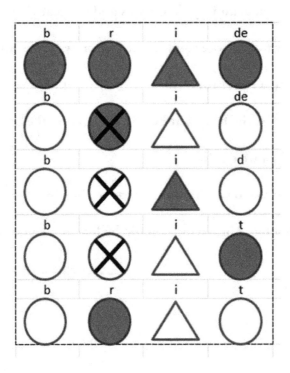

Another example:

When changing '**lamp**' to '**lap**' the /m/ is missing, so the second circle is marked.
Then when changing '**lap**' to '**lip**' the /m/ is still missing, so an **X** is placed in the second circle and the second space is marked because the /a/ is now /i/.
When changing '**lip**' to '**limp**', the /m/ is added back so the second circle is marked.

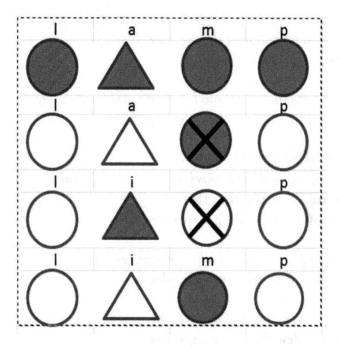

CCV ALL CONSONANT SOUNDS WITH LONG VOWELS IN /s/ BLENDS,

List One: long f, p, k with long/i/ and /a/- *long vowel final —y-:*
fly, ply, play, pray, fray, fry, cry, cray, clay, lay

List Two: s blends with long /i/, /a/ /o/, and /u/- *long vowel final —y, -ay, -ow, -ew:*
sty, spy, spay, stay, stew, stow, snow, slow, slew, spew

List Three: b, p, f with long /i/, /o/, /u/, and /a/-
long vowel final —ew, -ay, -ow; and long vowel —ew, -o, -ow, -y, final e:
brew, bray, ray, fray, fro, flow, foe, few, flew, fly
flew, blue, brew, bro, blow, flow, fro, pro, pry, fry

List Four: b, p, f, t with long /i/, /a/, and /e/ - *-ay, -ow, -ew, -ee, -ea:*
bray, pray, pre, plea, flee, free, tree, tea, pea, plea

List Five: s, f, t, d with long /i/, /o/, and /u/ - *-y, -ow, -ew, final e:*
sly, slow, slew, flew, few, dew, drew, true, try, dry

List Six: th, k, f with long /i/ /o/ /u/ /a/ /e/ - *-ow, -y, -ee, -ough, -ew:*
throw, crow, cry, fry, free, three, through, cue, crew, threw

List Seven: d, t, th, f, s with long /i/ /o/ /u/ /a/ /e/ - *-y —ee, -ay, -ow:*
dry, try, tree, three, free, fray, ray, say, slay, slow

List Eight: k, g with long /i/ /o/ /u/ /a/ /e/- *-ay,- ew,-ay, -ow, -y, final e:*
clay, clue, glue, grew, gray, grow, crow, cry, crew, cue

List Nine: p, b, t, d with long /i/ /o/ /u/ /a/ /e/ *-ee, -ew, -aw, -y, -ay, final e:*
tree, true, drew, draw, dry, try, tray, bray, pray, play

List Ten: s with long /i/ /o/ /u/ /a/ /e/ - *ew, —ee,-ay, —y, —igh- -o, -ow:*
slew, slee, see, say, slay, sly, lie, sigh, so, slow, low

CCV ALL CONSONANT SOUNDS WITH /s/, /r/ AND /l/ BLENDS

Lists Twenty One through Thirty Reading Page

List One:
fly, ply, play, pray, fray, fry, cry, cray, clay, lay

List Two:
sty spy spay stay stew stow snow slow slew spew

List Three:
brew, bray, ray, fray, fro, flow, foe, few, flew, fly
flew, blue, brew, bro, blow, flow, fro, pro, pry, fry

List Four:
bray, pray, pre, plea, flee, free, tree, tea, pea, plea

List Five:
sly, slow, slew, flew, few, dew, drew, true, try, dry

List Six:
throw, crow, cry, fry, free, three, through, cue, crew, threw

List Seven:
dry, try, tree, three, free, fray, ray, say, slay, slow

List Eight:
clay, clue, glue, grew, gray, grow, crow, cry, crew, cue

List Nine:
tree, true, drew, draw, dry, try, tray, bray, pray, play

List Ten:
slew, slee, see, say, slay, sly, lie, sigh, so, slow, low

CCV ALL CONSONANT SOUNDS WITH /s/, /r/ AND /l/ BLENDS

Sentences for Reading and Dictation

1. Fran likes to play with clay by the cray.

2. Stan ate a slew of stew in the snow.

3. Gram can brew blue tea like a pro.

4. The flea did plea to be free from the tree.

5. Is it true that he drew a spy with one eye?

6. Throw the crow through the crew of three on the ship.

7. Try to dry the wet fly and the flea.

8. The clay crow is gray and needs some glue.

9. He can try to draw a tree on the tray.

10. He was too slow to see what flew by the crow.

CCVC s BLENDS

Short Vowels and Long Vowels

List One: p, m, t, l in s blends with long and short vowel /i/: *final e, -ck, FLOSS, y for long i:*
stick, still, spill, pill, pile, tile, style, smile, mile, mill

ListTwo: p, n in s blends with long and short vowel /e/-[-ee-], -ea-], *final —ch and k:*
speech, speak, speck, sped, speed, seed, seek, sneak, sleek, leak

List Three: t, n, k in s blends with long and short vowel /a/- *final e, -ck:*
stake, stack, stag, snag, snap, sap, cap, cape, scape, scale

List Four: p, t, n, s in /s/ blends with long and short vowel /u/- [-oo-], [-al-], [-oo-], [-ou-]:
stun, spun, spoon, spool, stool, stoop, scoop, snoop, soup, soon

List Five: t, m in /s/ blends with long and short vowel /o/- *final e, [-al-] —ck:*
stove, stole, stall, stop, stock, stoke, smoke, smock, small, mall

List Six: /s/ blends with short vowels /a/, /u/ & /i/- *-dge, -tch, [-ee-]:*
smash, smush, smudge, smidge, Smith, smitch, snitch, snatch, snazz, sneeze

List Seven: /s/ blends with short vowels /i/ /e/:
slim, swim, switch, swill, swell, smell, spell, spill, spiff, sniff

List Eight: /s/ blends with long /i/, /a/ and /ee/- [-igh-], -ge, [-ee-], final e:
slight, slate, Slade, spade, speed, steed, steel, stale, state, stage

List Nine: /s/ blends with long /a/ /o/ /u/:
snub, snob, snot, slot, slat, slap, slop, stop, snop, snap

ListTen: s blends with long /ee/ /i/ /o/ - [-ea-], [-ee-], *final e, y for long i:*
steam, steep, sleep, slope, scope, skype, snipe, swipe, sweep

CCVC s BLENDS

Short Vowels and Long Vowels

Lists One through Ten Reading Page

List One:
stick, still, spill, pill, pile, tile, style, smile, mile, mill

ListTwo:
speech, speak, speck, sped, speed, seed, seek, sneak, sleek, leak

List Three:
stake, stack, stag, snag, snap, sap, cap, cape, scape, scale

List Four
stun, spun, spoon, spool, stool, stoop, scoop, snoop, soup, soon

List Five:
stove, stole, stall, stop, stock, stoke, smoke, smock, small, mall

List Six:
smash, smush, smudge, smidge, Smith, smitch, snitch, snatch, snazz, sneeze

List Seven:
slim, swim, switch, swill, swell, smell, spell, spill, spiff, sniff

List Eight:
slight, slate, Slade, spade, speed, steed, steel, stale, state, stage

List Nine:
snub, snob, snot, slot, slat, slap, slop, stop, snop, snap

ListTen:
steam, steep, sleep, slope, scope, skype, snipe, swipe, sweep

CCVC s BLENDS

Short Vowels and Long Vowels

Sentences for Reading and Dictation

1. She picked up a stick and put it in a pile by the mill with a smile.

2. His sleek steed ran with speed to sneak up on the spy in the far land.

3. Put a stake on the cape and add to the stack by the scale.

4. Spoon the soup by the stoop for the snoop on the stool.

5. The smoke on the stove came from the stock in the pot.

6. Mr. Smith can sneeze with snazz and smash a smidge of the stash.

7. Slim Jim can sniff, swim, spell and swell really well.

8. His steed is slate gray like the color of a steel spade.

9. Watch the snob stop to snub the boy with snot on his face.

10. The wind will sweep the steam up the steep slope.

CCVC l BLENDS

Short Vowels and Long Vowels

List Eleven: /l/ blends with short /i/ - -ck:
flit, fit, sit, slit, slip, lip, lid, slid, slick, lick

List Twelve: /l/ blends and short /e/- FLOSS, -dge, -ck:
pledge, ledge, fledge, fleck, bleck, bless, less, led, bled, fled

List Thirteen: /l/ blends and short /a/:- -ck, silent b:
flat, flag, lag, sag, slag, slack, sack, Sam, slam, lamb

List Fourteen: /l/ blends and short /u/ FLOSS, -ck:
pluck, luck, lug, plug, plum, plus, pus, fuss, fush, flush

List Fifteen: /l/ blends and short /o/- -ck:
plot, plog, log, lock, clock, cock, cog, clog, blog, bog

List Sixteen: /s/ /f/ /l/ /p/ in /l/ blends with long and short vowel /i/- -ck, [-igh-]:
slick, flick, flit, flight, fight, light, plight, slight, slit, slim

List Seventeen: /s/ /b/ /f/ /l/ in L blends with long and short vowel /e/- [-ee-], -dge:
sleek, sleep, bleep, bleem, blem, bled, fled, flesh, fledge, sledge

List Eighteen: /f/ /k/ /s/ /g/ in /l/ blends with long and short vowel /a/- finale e:
flap, flag, flash, clash, clam, claim, blame, lame, flame, fame

List Nineteen: /p/ /b/ /g/ /f/ in /l/ blends with long and short vowel /u/- final e, [-oo-]:
plume, bloom, bloop, gloop, glup, plup, pluck, plush, flush, flub

List Twenty: /k/ /s/ /b/ /f/ in /l/ blends with long and short vowel /o/- final e, [-oa-], -ck, [-ow-]:
clock, clog, slog, blog, block, bloke, blown, flown, Sloan, slope

CCVC l BLENDS

Short Vowels and Long Vowels Lists

Eleven through Twenty Reading Page

List Eleven:
flit, fit, sit, slit, slip, lip, lid, slid, slick, lick

List Twelve:
pledge, ledge, fledge, fleck, bleck, bless, less, led, bled, fled

List Thirteen:
flat, flag, lag, sag, slag, slack, sack, Sam, slam, lamb

List Fourteen:
pluck, luck, lug, plug, plum, plus, pus, fuss, fush, flush

List Fifteen:
plot, plog, log, lock, clock, cock, cog, clog, blog, bog

List Sixteen:
slick, flick, flit, flight, fight, light, plight, slight, slit, slim

List Seventeen:
sleek, sleep, bleep, bleem, blem, bled, fled, flesh, fledge, sledge

List Eighteen:
flap, flag, flash, clash, clam, claim, blame, lame, flame, fame

List Nineteen:
plume, bloom, bloop, gloop, glup, plup, pluck, plush, flush, flub

List Twenty:
clock, clog, slog, blog, block, bloke, blown, flown, Sloan, slope

CCVC I BLENDS

Short Vowels and Long Vowels

Sentences for Reading and Dictation

1. The bird flit and slid on the slick lid.

2. I pledge to stay on the ledge to bless the ones who fled.

3. The flat flag will sag so give it some slack to blow in the wind.

4. Pluck a plum from the tree and use it to plug the hole.

5. The cock will plod to the log and crow when the clock strikes three.

6. The man on the flight saw a slight flick of light through the slit in the cloud.

7. The sleek sheep fled and tried to bleat in his sleep.

8. The glam clams moved with a flash before they could clash with the slugs.

9. Pluck the plume of the bloom for the gloop.

10. Sloan will clog and slog up the slope before the bloke can make the clock chime.

CCVC r BLENDS

Short Vowels and Long Vowels

List Twenty -One: /r/ blends short vowel i – *FLOSS:*
Brit, brig, frig, rig, trig, trip, trill, drill, drip, dip

Twenty-Two: /r/ blends with short vowel e- *FLOSS, [-ea-], [-ch for k]:*
dress, press, prep, rep, red, dread, tread, Ted, tech, trek

Twenty-Three: /r/ blends with short vowel a *FLOSS:*
bass, brass, crass, crab, grab, gab, dab, drab, drag, rag

List Twenty Four: /r/ blends short vowel u- *FLOSS, -ck:*
from, drum, drug, rug, tug, tuck, truck, truss, Russ, gruss

List Twenty-Five: /r/ blends short vowel o – *[-augh-]:*
cross, Ross, rod, trod, prod, pod, pog, fog, frog, fraught

List Twenty-Six: /g/ /p/ /b/ /f/ in /r/ blends with long and short vowel /i/ - *final e, FLOSS:*
grip, grim, grime, prime, prim, brim, brick, brig, frig, frill

List Twenty-Seven: /g/ /d/ /l/ /t/ in /r/ blends with long and short vowel /e/- *FLOSS, [-ea-]:*
Greg, reg, dreg, dress, press, tress, trek, wreck, wreak, freak

List Twenty Eight: /k/ /f/ /g/ /b/ /t/ in /r/ blends with long and short vowel /a/- *final e, [-ai-], -ck:*
cram, Fram, frame, frail, grail, brail, brake, brack, brash, trash

List Twenty-Nine: /sh/ /g/ /b/ /k/ in /r/ blends with long and short vowel /u/- *-dge, [-oo-], [-ue-]:*
shrug, shrub, grub, grudge, grum, groom, broom, brool, cruel, cool

List Thirty: /d/ /p/ /f/ /b/ /k/ in /r/ blends with long and short vowel /o/- *-ck, final e, [-oa-]:*
drop, prop, prom, prog, frog, frock, brock, broke, croak, crock

CCVC r BLENDS

Short Vowels and Long Vowels

Lists Twenty One through Thirty Reading Page

List Twenty-One:
Brit, brig, frig, rig, trig, trip, trill, drill, drip, dip

Twenty Two:
dress, press, prep, rep, red, dread, tread, Ted, tech, trek

Twenty-Three:
bass, brass, crass, crab, grab, gab, dab, drab, drag, rag

List Twenty-Four:
from, drum, drug, rug, tug, tuck, truck, truss, Russ, gruss

List Twenty-Five:
cross, Ross, rod, trod, prod, pod, pog, fog, frog, fraught

List Twenty-Six:
grip, grim, grime, prime, prim, brim, brick, brig, frig, frill

List Twenty-Seven:
Greg, reg, dreg, dress, press, tress, trek, wreck, wreak, freak

List Twenty-Eight:
cram, Fram, frame, frail, grail, brail, brake, brack, brash, trash

List Twenty-Nine:
shrug, shrub, grub, grudge, grum, groom, broom, brool, cruel, cool

List Thirty:
drop, prop, prom, prog, frog, frock, brock, broke, croak, crock

CCVC r BLENDS

Short Vowels and Long Vowels

Sentences for Reading and Dictation

1. Brit got on the frig to take a trip.

2. Jen put on a red dress to tread the path on her long trek.

3. The bass swam through the brass ring by the crag.

4. Russ could hear the drum of the truck rolling on the road.

5. Ross the frog fought his way to cross the road.

6. Grip the cup to fill it to the brim with your prime punch.

7. Greg can press the dress for the girl with a long tress.

8. Fran put the grail in the trash with the frame and the brake for the bike.

9. The groom will use the broom to sweep the shrub into the cool night.

10. The croak of the frog was a prop for the play.

CCVC r AND l BLENDS

Short Vowels and Long Vowels

List Thirty-One: r and l blends with long /i/ and /u/- *[drop the –y to add -ed]*, *[-igh-]*, *final e*:
bride, pride, dried, tried, fried, fright, bright, blight, flight, flute

List Thirty-Two: r and l blends with long /i/ and /a/ - *[-ay- with –ed]*, *final e*, *[-igh-]*, *[drop the –y to add -ed]*:
blade, played, prayed, trade, tried, pride, bride, bide, bite, bright

List Thirty Three: r and l blends with mixed long /i/,/e/ and /o/-*final e*, *[-igh-]*,*[-oa-]*,*[-ow-]*, *[-ee-]*:
lime, light, blight, bloat, float, flown, blown, bloat, bleat, bleed

List Thirty-Four: r and l blends with long /u/ and /oo/- *[-oo-]*, *final e*:
bloom, boom, broom, brute, root, Ruth, truth, true, troop, droop

List Thirty-Five: r and l blends with mixed long vowels – *[-ea-]*, *[-ee-]*:
dream, cream, creed, creep, keep, seep, sleep, bleep, blop, blob

List Thirty-Six: r and l blends with mixed long vowels – *final e*, *[-ai-]*, *[-ea-]*, *[-ee-]*:
prone, drone, drain, train, trail, trait, treat, greet, Crete, cleat

List Thirty-Seven: r and l blends with mixed long and short vowels – *[-augh, final e, [-oo-]*:
fraught, frog, frag, slag, slog, slug, plug, plum, plume, loom

List Thirty-Eight: /g/ /p/ /s/ in l blends with mixed long and short vowels – *final e*, *[-ay- with –ed]* *[-oo-]*, *[-ee-]*:
glade, played, plate, slate, sleet, slit, slip, slope, sloop, stoop

List Thirty-Nine: /b/ /t/ /d/ in /r/ blends with long /a/ and /o/ - *[-ai-]*, *final e*, *silent w*:
brave, rave, rove, wrote, rate, trait, train, drain, drone

List Forty: /d/ /t/ /b/ in /r/ blends with mixed long and short vowels – *[-ea-]*, *[-igh-]*, *[-ee-]*, *[-ough-]* *final e*:
dread, tread, bread, breed, bride, bright, Brit, brat, brought, trot

CCVC r AND l BLENDS

Short Vowels and Long Vowels

Lists Thirty One through Forty Reading Page

List Thirty-One:
bride, pride, dried, tried, fried, fright, bright, blight, flight, flute

List Thirty-Two:
blade, played, prayed, trade, tried, pride, bride, bide, bite, bright

List Thirty-Three:
lime, light, blight, bloat, float, flown, blown, bloat, bleat, bleed

List Thirty-Four:
bloom, boom, broom, brute, root, Ruth, truth, true, troop, droop

List Thirty-Five:
dream, cream, creed, creep, keep, seep, sleep, bleep, blop, blob

List Thirty-Six:
prone, drone, drain, train, trail, trait, treat, greet, Crete, cleat

List Thirty-Seven:
fraught, frog, frag, slag, slog, slug, plug, plum, plume, loom

List Thirty-Eight:
glade, played, plate, slate, sleet, slit, slip, slope, sloop, stoop

List Thirty-Nine:
brave, rave, rove, wrote, rate, trait, train, drain, drone

List Forty:
dread, tread, bread, breed, bride, bright, Brit, brat, brought, trot

CCVC r AND l BLENDS

Sentences for Reading and Dictation
for lists One through Ten

1. The bride played a bright tune on her flute with pride.

2. He will bide his time and trade his pride for a bright bride.

3. The boat did float and was blown into the lime light.

4. Ruth picked up the bloom with the broom.

5. At night Ruth did dream about true cream in her sleep.

6. The drone flew over Crete to greet the train.

7. The slug saw the frog loom near the plum.

8. He played in the glade near the slope with his slate.

9. The brave little train chugged over the drain.

10. Brit ate bread and brought some to his bright bride.

CVCC AND CCVCC

Lists One through Ten

List One: Labial & Alveolar & Dental -pt, -lm, -st with short e and long i– *[doubling consonants], adding –ed, FLOSS:*
kept, wept, wiped, whipped, wit, wet, west, Wes, well

List Two: Labial & Alveolar &, -p, -lt, -ld, --nd, -nt with short a and o - *silent w, [-al-], FLOSS, sight word 'was':*
wrap, rasp, wasp, was, wall, Walt, what, wad, wand,

List Three: Labial & Alveolar & Dental -st, -ld, -lf with short u and long o- *FLOSS, -ed, [-oa-] [long o with –st & –ld], {-short u as [-olf-] & [-oo-]}:*
wolf, wool, pull, pulled, polled, old, mold, mode, moat, most

List Four: Labial & Alveolar & Dental -mp, -sp, -ps, -ft with short u and i:
lump, limp, lisp, lips, sips, sip, sit, sift, lift

List Five: Alveolar and Dentals -st, -sk, -nk and the consonant phoneme/ng/ with short e and i:
pesk, peck, pick, pink, ink, link, rink, ring, writ, wrist

List Six: Alveolar and Dentals: -nd, -sk, -kt, -nk and the consonant phoneme/ ng/ with short a:
act, pact, pack, lack, lad, land, sand, sank, sang, Sal

List Seven: Alveolar and Dentals: -lt, -ld, -nd, -st with short o and long o-- *[-au-], [-al-], FLOSS, [-oa-], [-ol-]:*
salt, Saul, fall, foal, fold, cold, colt, coat, coast, toast

List Eight: Alveolar and Dentals: -lt, -ld, -nd, -nt, -lk with short u, i, e -- *FLOSS, [-ui-]:*
bulk, bilk, bill, built, bit, bet, belt, bent, sent, send

List Nine: all CVCC endings with /sh/ /ch/ /y/ and/th/ discrimination with short i, e and long i, e- *FLOSS, -ed, [-il-], final ee, [-ie-], contraction with 'will':*
Chilled, child, chimed, chide, shied, shelled, yelled, yield, shield, she'll

List Ten: all CVCC endings with /sh/ /ch/ /y/ /th/discrimination and /r/ blends with diphthongs- *-or-, -ir-, -ear-, -ar-:*
Short, shirt, shirp, chirp, churn, yearn, yarn, yard, shard, chard

CVCC AND CCVCC

Lists One through Ten

Lists One through Ten Reading Page

List One:
kept, wept, wiped, whipped, wit, wet, west, Wes, well

List Two:
wrap, rasp, wasp, was, wall, Walt, what, wad, wand,

List Three:
wolf, wool, pull, pulled, polled, old, mold, mode, moat, most

List Four:
lump, limp, lisp, lips, sips, sip, sit, sift, sift

List Five:
pesk, peck, pick, pink, ink, link, rink, ring, writ, wrist

List Six:
act, pact, pack, lack, lad, land, sand, sank, sang, Sal

List Seven:
salt, Saul, fall, foal, fold, cold, colt, coat, coast, toast

List Eight:
bulk, bilk, bill, built, bit, bet, belt, bent, sent, send

List Nine:
Chilled, child, chimed, chide, shied, shelled, yelled, yield, shield, she'll

List Ten:
Short, shirt, shirp, chirp, churn, yearn, yarn, yard, shard, chard

CVCC AND CCVCC

Sentences for Reading and Dictation

1. She wept and wiped the wet whipped cream off her face.

2. Walt took the wand and put it in a wad of wrap.

3. The wolf pulled the old wool over his back.

4. The lump on the old man's back made him limp.

5. Pick up the pink ink pen and draw a link from one ring to the other.

6. Sal acted and sang on the land that sank in the sand.

7. He named his colt Saul because it looked like salt from the coast.

8. He built a bent hulk with the bulk of the sand that you sent.

9. The child chilled the shelled nuts while the bell chimed.

10. The short grandma can churn butter in the yard while the birds chirp.

CVCC AND CCVCC

Lists Eleven through Twenty

List Eleven: s, l, d, with nasal blends -mp, -nd, - nk, consonant ng with short e, a, u:
send, said, sud, sup, sump, lump, lamp, lap, Lang, lank

List Twelve: s, l with nasal blends -mp, -nd, - nk with short a, u, i *–silent b:*
sand, sank, sunk, sun, sum, sump, lump, limp, limb, lamb

List Thirteen: l, t, ch, and s blends with nasal blend -mp using short a, u, o:
lap, lamp, tamp, stamp, stump, sump, chump, champ, chomp, chop

List Fourteen: k, t, d, l with -rd, -rt, -rn, -rk – *using diphthongs for [-or-], [-ar-]:*
cork, corn, cord, card, cart, part, park, lark, lard, Lord

List Fifteen: p, b, f, t with -rt, -rp, -rm, -rn,-rk – *using diphthongs for [-ur-], [-er-], [-or-]:*
burp, burn, berm, firm, fir, for, fork, form, fort, port

List Sixteen: s blends and nasal blends [-sp, -nt,-nd, -ld] in CCVCC, CCVC and CVCC -*FLOSS, -ed, doubling consonants, -ed, FLOSS:*
spend, spent, sent, send, sand, spanned, spinned, spilled, spill, sill

List Seventeen: s blends and nasal blends [-sp, -nt,-nd, -kt] in CCVCC, CCVC and CVCC– *ed, -ck, [-oa-]:*
sacked, smacked, smoked, soaked, stoked, staked, stacked, stack, Stan, stand

List Eighteen: l blends and nasal blends [pl, bl, cl, nt, nd, nk] in CCVCC with CCVC and CVCC:
plant, planned, plank, blank, clank, clink, link, tink, think, thank

List Nineteen: r, s and nasal blends [dr, sk, sp, st, nk] in CVCC with CCVC and CVCC:
drank, drink, drunk, dunk, chunk, sunk, skunk, spunk, stunk, stink

List Twenty: r, s and nasal blends [shr, pr, pl, st, -nk, -nd] in CCVCC with CCVC and CVCC:
rink, shrink, shrank, prank, plank, lank, tank, stank, stand

CVCC AND CCVCC

Lists Eleven through Twenty Lists

Eleven through Twenty Reading Page

List Eleven:
send, said, sud, sup, sump, lump, lamp, lap, Lang, lank

List Twelve:
sand, sank, sunk, sun, sum, sump, lump, limp, limb, lamb

List Thirteen
lap, lamp, tamp, stamp, stump, sump, chump, champ, chomp, chop

List Fourteen:
cork, corn, cord, card, cart, part, park, lark, lard, Lord

List Fifteen:
burp, burn, berm, firm, fir, for, fork, form, fort, port

List Sixteen:
spend, spent, sent, send, sand, spanned, spinned, spilled, spill, sill

List Seventeen:
sacked, smacked, smoked, soaked, stoked, staked, stacked, stack, Stan, stand

List Eighteen:
plant, planned, plank, blank, clank, clink, link, tink, think, thank

List Nineteen:
drank, drink, drunk, dunk, chunk, sunk, skunk, spunk, stunk, stink

List Twenty:
rink, shrink, shrank, prank, plank, lank, tank, stank, stand

CVCC AND CCVCC

Sentences for Reading and Dictation
Lists Eleven through Twenty

1. The tall, lank lad sat like a lump on the land by the sump pump.

2. The lamb sank in the sand as the sun sunk.

3. He tried to stomp out the fire made by the lamp when the champ tried to chop the stump.

4. The card shows part of a park with corn growing and a lark singing.

5. They built a fort near the port to keep the form from burning.

6. He spent more for the spilled milk than he spent for the sand by the sill.

7. Stan sacked the food and stoked the fire until it smoked.

8. I think the link between the clank and the clink is a blank plank.

9. He drank his drink until the skunk stunk.

10. The child played a prank that made the tank by the rink start to stink.

AFTERWORD

In 1990, I found a copy of the Lindamood Auditory Conceptualization Test [LAC] in the speech therapy room closet. The background research and information contained in the books supporting the LAC test fascinated me. Then, in 1994, I attended a workshop presented by Nanci Bell at the Madisonville Children's Home in Cincinnati, Ohio.

During the workshop on Visualizing and Verbalizing, Nanci Bell took a detour and began to tell about the Auditory Discrimination in Depth program [known as the LIPS program today]. She explained how it was developed, what it did and a little about how to implement the strategies.

After purchasing the ADD program and combing through manuals that came with it, I discovered that, as early as the 1940s, researchers were studying and confirming the need for phonemic awareness for developing decoding skills and fluent reading. The research documented that approximately 30% of the population needed direct, explicit instruction in the basic sound units of words, sound to letter associations, and phonics in order to become fluent readers and spellers.

In the early 2000's Dr. Kenn Apel [Learning by Design] presented at a winter conference for SWOSLHA [South West Ohio Speech Language-Hearing Association] workshop. In 2003, Dr. Jan Wasowicz presented for an OSSPEAC [Ohio Schools Speech Pathology and Audiology Coalition] conference. Their presentations explained the link between phonemic understanding and classroom skills; they further explained how to assess, and how to provide treatment. During the 1990's Dr. Reid Lyon of National Institute of Health wrote on the same topic. Good Housekeeping magazine {October, 1994 page 124} even contained an article on the topic suggesting that parents should seek out the help of a speech language pathologist if they suspected dyslexia in their child. I knew that I needed to learn more on this topic.

The journey began in 1990, and new information was continually collected over the next several years. All of the ideas presented from the various sources connected. The ADD program was invaluable and rich with materials, strategies, and instructions for addressing the needs for this population. I then began to seek further knowledge by attending Dyslexia conferences at the Springer School in Cincinnati, Ohio. The speakers at the Dyslexia conferences enriched the information already acquired. The conclusion was clear: Teach children using a multisensory approach to segment, sequence and blend sounds. Teach them to map sounds to letters. Teach them to connect sound patterns to letter patterns and they will learn to read fluently, write fluently and spell accurately.

Classroom communication requires fluent speaking, listening, reading and writing skills. Students cannot discuss curriculum in texts or answer questions about what they read unless they can fluently decode the written word. Then, at about the same time, ASHA posted a statement supporting the role of the SLP in the area of phonemic and phonological processing

There is an old proverb that says, "If you are a hammer, every problem needs a nail." Within the area of education each professional has his or her own 'hammer' and 'nail' for teaching reading, writing, and spelling skills. Traditionally, the SLP has not been considered as a resource for supporting reading, writing or spelling. Additionally, SLP caseloads are usually quite large, approaching or exceeding 70 to 80 students further limiting the time an SLP may allocate to servicing phonemic processing needs. While the need was obvious to me, it was also apparent that application of knowledge would not be an easy task.

The earliest attempt came in the form of block scheduling in short terms [40 minutes a week for 6 weeks, then 20 minutes a week for 12] {middle 1990's}. Excellent results were achieved. Students were gaining one to two years growth in reading skill development within one semester, but most administrators and staff believed the benefits came through the classroom and believed the therapy time interfered with amount of exposure to classroom curriculum [their 'hammer and nail'.]. Free after school therapy provided from time to time yielded markedly better results than 30 minutes a week during the day, and summer time therapy with free or reduced price yielded a year's growth within six weeks. However, each attempt to address the time issues was blocked by bureaucratic or ethical barriers.

I was unable to communicate the value of intense SLP intervention so that educational professionals were willing to give up instructional time and administrators would be interested in devoting therapist resources to this treatment. The only real answer was to find a means of providing the training in shorter segments of time, targeted to specific areas of need and delivered in short sessions over the course of a school year.

The exercises in *20 Minute Phonemic Training for Dyslexia, Auditory Processing, and Spelling* are the result of many years of observation and learning from research and my students. It is my hope, for the sake of our children, that other professionals will read the medical research being released today supporting the advantage of brain plasticity to develop neural pathways between the nodes of the brain that enable individuals to decode and encode the written word. The articles and online workshops noted in the bibliography, particularly those by Dr. Martha Burns, explain the latest research especially well.

APPENDIX A

Informal Spelling Assessment

CVC List 1

1. van
2. pit
3. mix
4. rob
5. chum
6. mesh
7. chip
8. shut
9. thug
10. Beth
11. hide
12. rode
13. gap
14. wave
15. gape
16. sheet
17. cot
18. feed
19. cut
20. zit
21. boss
22. fed
23. sun
24. nip
25. buzz
26. file
27. bill
28. mute
29. wove
30. cute

CCVC List 2

1. black
2. brake
3. flake
4. stack
5. track
6. brand
7. snake
8. strand
9. drug
10. snug
11. plot
12. trick
13. click
14. spend
15. plant
16. split
17. spunk
18. blessed
19. fret
20. crest
21. clunk
22. drink
23. fling
24. glad
25. print
26. grand
27. crack
28. scold
29. swung
30. slips
31. lists
32. smoke
33. husk
34. frump
35. slump
36. glob
37. prize
38. grape
39. smack
40. skunk

List 3
Two Syllable Words
With –le and
Consonant doubling

1. humble
2. pickle
3. cuddle
4. brittle
5. thimble
6. rattle
7. dazzle
8. bottle
9. fable
10. bugle
11. bible
12. table
13. maple
14. candle
15. handle
16. rustle
17. raffle
18. cripple
19. settle
20. jungle
21. cradle
22. bridle
23. staple
24. ruffle
25. buckle
26. drizzle

CVC Assessment Grid   Check the student errors
against the categories of sounds to see if a trend is present.
For example, if they consistently miss a particular short vowel sound,
or confuse /t/ and /d/ sounds.

	Labial	Alveolar	Dental	Palatal	Velar	Voiced/ Voiceless	Blends	short i	short e	short a	short u	short o	long e	long a	long o	long u	long i
van		x	x			x				x							
pit	x	x				x		x									
mix	x				x	x		x									
rob	x			x		x						x					
chum	x			x		x					x						
mesh	x			x		x			x								
chip	x			x		x		x									
shut		x		x		x					x						
thug			x		x	x					x						
Beth	x		x	x		x			x								
hide		x			x	x											x
rode		x		x		x									x		
gap	x				x	x				x							
wave	x		x			x								x			
gape	x				x	x								x			
sheet		x		x		x							x				
cot		x			x	x						x					
feed		x	x			x							x				
cut		x			x	x					x						
zit		x				x		x									
boss	x	x				x											
fed		x	x			x			x								
sun		x				x					x						
nip	x	x				x		x									
buzz	x	x				x					x						
file		x	x			x											x
bill	x	x				x		x									
mute	x	x				x										x	
wove	x		x			x									x		
cute		x			x	x										x	

CCVC - CVCC - CCVCC Assessment Grid   Check the student errors
against the categories of sounds to see if a trend is present.
For example, if they consistently miss a particular short vowel sound,
omit /l/ in blends, or confuse /t/ and /d/ sounds.

	Labial	Alveolar	Dental	Palatal	Velar	Voiced/ Voiceless	Blends	short i	short e	short a	short u	short o	long e	long a	long o	long u	long i
black	x	x			x	x	x			x							
brake	x			x	x	x	x							x			
flake		x	x		x	x	x							x			
stack		x			x	x	x			x							
track		x		x	x	x	x			x							
brand	x	x		x		x	x			x							
snake		x			x	x	x							x			
strand		x		x		x	x			x							
drug		x		x	x	x	x				x						
snug		x			x	x	x				x						
plot	x	x				x	x					x					
trick		x		x	x	x	x	x									
click		x			x	x	x	x									
spend	x	x				x	x		x								
plant	x	x				x	x			x							
split	x	x				x	x	x									
spunk	x	x			x	x	x				x						
blest	x	x				x	x		x								
fret		x	x	x		x	x		x								
crest		x		x	x	x	x		x								
clunk		x			x	x	x				x						
drink		x		x	x	x	x	x									
fling		x	x	x		x	x	x									
glad		x			x	x	x			x							
print	x	x		x		x	x	x									
grand		x		x	x	x	x			x							
crack		x		x	x	x	x			x							
scold		x			x	x	x								x		
swung	x	x			x	x	x				x						
slips	x	x				x	x	x									
lists		x				x	x	x									
smoke	x	x			x	x	x								x		
husk		x			x	x	x				x						
frump	x	x	x	x		x	x				x						
thump	x	x	x			x	x				x						
glob	x	x			x	x	x					x					
prize	x	x				x	x										x
grape	x			x	x	x	x							x			
smack	x	x			x	x	x			x							
skunk		x			x	x	x				x						

APPENDIX B

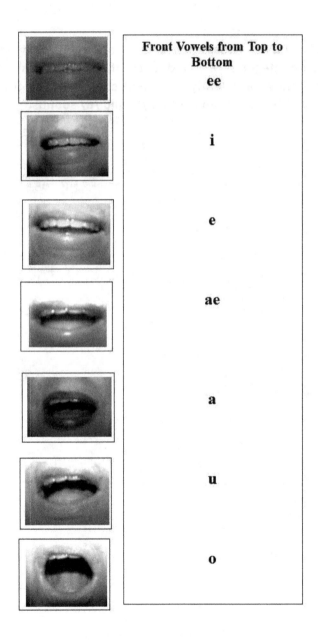

Front Vowels from Top to Bottom

ee

i

e

ae

a

u

o

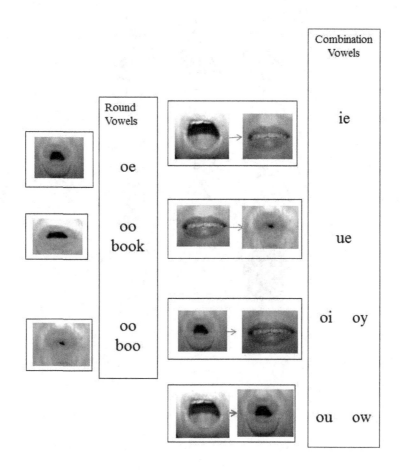

APPENDIX C

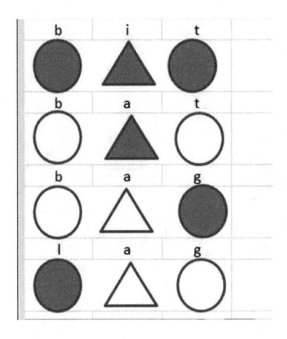

STUDENT WORK
PAGE CVC

WRITING PRACTICE

1._____

2._____

3._____

4._____

5._____

6._____

7._____

8._____

9._____

10._____

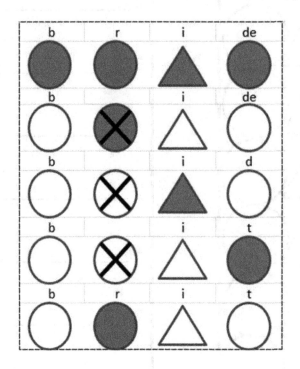

STUDENT WORK
PAGE CCV

WRITING PRACTICE

1._____

2._____

3._____

4._____

5._____

6._____

7._____

8._____

9._____

10._____

STUDENT WORK
PAGE CCVC

WRITING PRACTICE

1._____

2._____

3._____

4._____

5._____

6._____

7._____

8._____

9._____

10._____

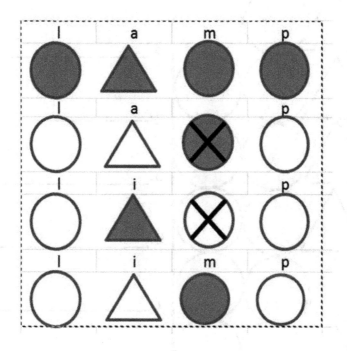

STUDENT WORK
PAGE CVCC

WRITING PRACTICE

1._____

2._____

3._____

4._____

5._____

6._____

7._____

8._____

9._____

10._____

STUDENT WORK
PAGE CCVCC

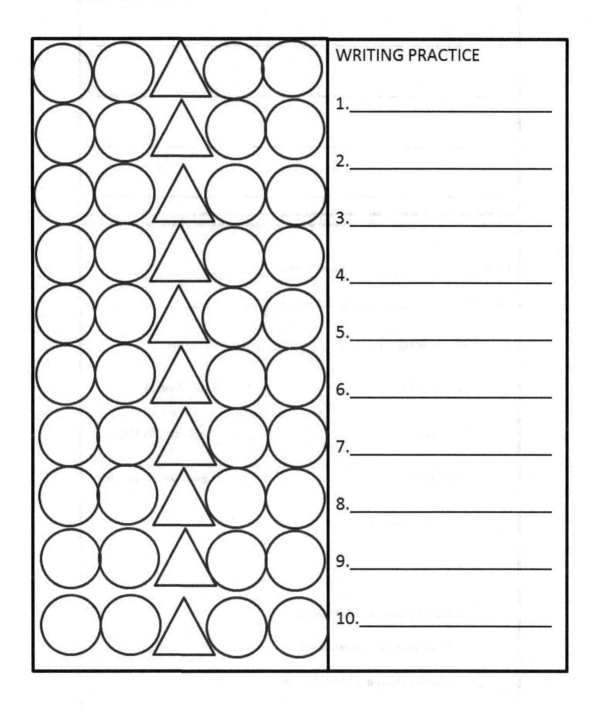

WRITING PRACTICE

1._____

2._____

3._____

4._____

5._____

6._____

7._____

8._____

9._____

10._____

Observational Notes:

_____

_____

_____

_____

_____

Date_____/_____/_____   Student Name:_____

List Name_____

_____/10 Auditory Tracking   _____/10   Reading

_____/10   Blending   _____/10 Word Writing

_____/10 Segmenting   _____/___ Sentence Writing

_____/10 Deletions   _____/10 Phoneme reversals

_____/10 Rhyme detection

_____/10 Rhyme generation

_____/10 Initial phoneme identification

_____/10 Final phoneme identification

_____/10 Medial phoneme identification

APPENDIX D

SHORT VOWEL PHONIC RULES
Sound for the Letter Name is turned OFF

1. There is NO /e/ on the end of the syllable. *can, ten, kit, not, cut*

2. FLOSS When the last sound is /f/ /l/ or /s/, there will usually be two of them. *The word FLOSS is a mnemonic to help remember the rule. FLOSS contains all three sounds, has a short vowel and two 's' letters on the end.* *hill, fell, cuff, mess, stuff, boss* *Common exceptions: bus, gas, us, yes*

3. When the last sound in a one syllable syllable is /k/, it is spelled –ck *tack, check, lick, smock*

4. When /ch/ is on the end of a one syllable syllable, it is usually spelled –tch or -nch. *match, butch, pitch, punch, pinch* *Common exceptions include: rich much, such, which*

5. When the final sound in a one syllable syllable is /j/, it will be spelled –dge. *Mudge, hedge, ridge, badge, budge*

6. When a one syllable or two-syllable word has a short vowel and: *you are adding an ending beginning with a vowel after the vowel THEN: double the last consonant to keep the first syllable closed and the vowel short. *hop / hopping big / biggest mop / mopped*

7. When a two-syllable syllable ends with a short vowel and one consonant, double the final consonant as in number 6. *ruf fle / ruffled / ruffling*

8. When you spell a two syllable word and the first syllable has a short vowel, there is usually a consonant at the end of the first syllable & one at the beginning of the second syllable. [the first syllable is closed] *lit tle hap pen sud den lic king sup per din ner mus tard*

LONG VOWEL PHONIC RULES
Sound for the Letter Name is turned ON

1. An /e/ on the end of the syllable is one of three ways to make a vowel turn 'on.' *cane, teen, note, cute* Note: long /e/ letters often stay together *weed, seed, feed*

2. When a vowel is long, you do not add two /l/ /f/ or /s/ letters at the end, just add the final /e/. *lake, pile fuse feel pose race** [*note that sometimes –ce is used to maintain the /s/ sound from becoming a /z/ sound when pronounced]

3. When the final sound is /k/ just add an /e/ to the end. DO NOT USE –ck. *Take, cheek, like, smoke, duke*

4. A double letter vowel spelling is used for the long vowel before the /ch/. *Each, reach, coach,*

5. When the final sound in a one syllable syllable is /j/, it is spelled –ge. /J/ is never used as the last letter in an English syllable. *Huge, change, page, gage*

6. When a one syllable word has a long vowel, drop the /e/ and add -ing, -ed, -est, or –er. *facing, faced, racer, piling, piled, taped, taping* When a two syllable word has a long vowel in the first syllable, there will only be one consonant between the vowel in the first and second syllables. This allows the first syllable to be an open syllable and is the second way a long vowel sound is created in a syllable. *ma ple ba by di ner su per*

7. When the second syllable in a two syllable syllable has a long vowel sound, do not double the final consonant. *Admire / admiring / admired*

8. When you spell a two syllable word and the first syllable has a long vowel, there will not be a consonant at the end of the first syllable to keep the syllable open and make the vowel long. *Li king, super, ru dest, fi nal, re sist*

APPENDIX E

Phonic Rules Word Lists

FLOSS RULE

toss - toes
bass - base
bell,
chill
boss
hill
dull - duel
pill -pile
full - fuel
gull
loss
lass- lace
lull
mull- mule
sell -seal
shell
tell - teal
skull
skill
mess
dress
glass
miss - mice
shall -shale
moss
fuss
brass - brace
press
stress
gloss
across
fess

bull
chess -cheese
guess
stuff
scuff
cuff
fluff
bluff

-ck RULE

back - bake
tack - take
rack - rake
lack – lake
sack – sake
lick – like
tick – tyke
Mick – Mike
pick – pike
check – cheek
peck – peek
beck – beak
puck – puke
duck – Duke
luck - Luke
slick
thick
neck
deck
kick
sick
chick
stick

flick
fleck
brick
block
pluck
broke
coke
soak
joke
fake
cake
make
seek
meek
leak
puke
poke

-tch RULE

hatch
patch
match
batch
thatch
latch
catch
pitch
ditch
hitch
mitch
witch
fetch
notch

scratch
hutch
peach
teach
reach
beach
each
coach
poach
roach
pooch

-dge RULE
edge
ledge
fudge
judge
dodge
pledge
bridge
badge
lodge
budge
ridge
sludge
wedge
stage
cage
wage
huge
page

THE –le SYLLABLE AND CONSONANT DOUBLING
pull – pulling – pulled
fill – filling –filled
file –filing
slide – sliding
ride – riding
hop – hopping – hopped
hope –hoping –hoped

rope –roping –roped
rip –ripping –ripped
fit –fitting –fitted
like –liking –liked
lick –licking –licked
fail –failing –failed
strike- striking
dinner –diner
bitter- biter
holly –holy
rudder –ruder
super –supper
mopping –moping
fitting –fighting
setting – seating
tipping –typing
little
fiddle
riddle
paddle
tattle
cradle
table
maple
staple
waggle
chuckle
buckle
tickle
cycle
circle
purple

-ce ENDING
ace
face
pace
race
ice
rice
mice
nice

dice
thrice
slice
price

-all ENDING
all
call
tall
wall
fall
mall
ball

-old ENDING
cold
sold
old
mold
hold
told
fold
gold

-olt ENDING
bolt
jolt
dolt
colt
volt

-ose SOUNDS LIKE /z
nose
rose
hose
pose
dose

OPEN and CLOSED SYLLABLES
me - met
she - shell

go - tot	**TWO SOUNDS OF –ED**	noted
a - at	**/d/**	netted
so - sog	weeded	pinned
be - bet	wooded	pined
we - wet	webbed	boated
din-ner -- di-ner	whined	**/t/**
tab –let -- ta-ble	pleaded	whipped
bit-ter – bi –t er	boomed	wiped
hol-ly – ho-ly	beamed	pooped
fil –ling – fi-ling	dined	piped
hop-ping – ho-ping	tuned	popped
	needed	topped
	named	napped

APPENDIX F

Sample Goals

Given five each CVC words, xxx will spell 80% of the words correctly on two samples
Given five each CCVC words, xxx will spell 80% of the words correctly on two samples
Given five each CVCC words, xxx will spell 80% of the words correctly on two samples

Given three minutes and a topic xxx will write a paragraph spelling 80% of the CVC words written correctly on two samples.
Given three minutes and a topic xxx will write a paragraph spelling 80% of the CCVC words written correctly on two samples
Given three minutes and a topic xxx will write a paragraph spelling 80% of the CVCC words written correctly on two samples

Given ten CVC words, student will correctly decode 80% on two samples
Given ten CCVC words, student will correctly decode 80% on two samples
Given ten CVCC words, student will correctly decode 80% on two samples

Given five sentences containing primarily CVC words, student will correctly decode 80% on two samples
Given five sentences containing primarily CCVC words, student will correctly decode 80% on two samples
Given five sentences containing primarily CVCC words, student will correctly decode 80% on two samples

Given ten CVC words, student will correctly spell 80% on two samples
Given ten CCVC words, student will correctly spell 80% on two samples
Given ten CVCC words, student will correctly spell 80% on two samples

Given five sentences containing primarily CVC words, student will correctly encode 80% on two samples
Given five sentences containing primarily CCVC words, student will correctly encode 80% on two samples
Given five sentences containing primarily CVCC words, student will correctly encode 80% on two samples

Sample Objectives

Given five CVC words student will segment, delete one sound to create a new word,
Given five words student will change one sound to create a new word,
Given five CVC words student will spell 4 of 5 of the words correctly on two samples
Given ten CVC words student will correctly track the phoneme changes on 8 of 10 on two samples.

Given five CCVC words student will segment, delete one sound to create a new word,
Given five CCVC words student will change one sound to create a new word,
Given five CCVC words student will spell 4 of 5 of the words correctly on two samples
Given ten CCVC words student will correctly track the phoneme changes on 8 of 10 on two samples.

Given five CVCC words student will segment, delete one sound to create a new word,
Given five CVCC words student will change one sound to create a new word,
Given five CVCC words student will spell 4 of 5 of the words correctly on two samples
Given ten CVCC words student will correctly track the phoneme changes on 8 of 10 on two samples.

Given five CCVC words student will segment, delete one sound to create a new word, change one sound to create a new word, and spell 80% of the words correctly on two samples
Given five CVCC words student will segment, delete one sound to create a new word, change one sound to create a new word, and spell 80% of the words correctly on two samples

Given five short vowel words ending with the /k/ sound, the student will spell four of five correctly on two samples.
Given five long vowel words ending with the /k/ sound, the student will spell 4 of 5 correctly on two samples.
Given five mixed vowel words ending with the /k/ sound, the student will spell 4 of 5 correctly on two samples

Given five short vowel words ending with the /ch/ sound, the student will spell 4 of 5 correctly on two samples.
Given five long vowel words ending with the /ch/ sound, the student will spell 4 of 5 correctly on two samples.
Given five mixed vowel words ending with the /ch/ sound, the student will spell 4 of 5 correctly on two samples

Given five short vowel words ending with the /j/ sound, the student will spell 4 of 5 correctly on two samples.

Given five long vowel words ending with the /j / sound, the student will spell 4 of 5 correctly on two samples.

Given five mixed vowel words ending with the /j/ sound, the student will spell 4 of 5 correctly on two samples

Given five CVC words student will delete one sound to create a new word correctly for 4 of 5 words on two samples

Given five CCVC words student will delete one sound to create a new word correctly for 4 of 5 words on two samples

Given five CVCC words student will delete one sound to create a new word correctly for 4 of 5 words on two samples

Given five sets of segmented CVC phonemes student will repeat and blend the phonemes to figure out the word correctly for 4 of 5 on two samples by the end of the IEP cycle.

Given five sets of segmented CCVC phonemes student will repeat and blend the phonemes to figure out the word correctly for 4 of 5 on two samples by the end of the IEP cycle

Given five sets of segmented CVCC phonemes student will repeat and blend the phonemes to figure out the word correctly for 4 of 5 on two samples by the end of the IEP cycle

GLOSSARY

alphabetic principle: the concept that letters and patterns of letters are symbols that represent sounds

alveolar: sounds produced when the tongue touches or is in close proximity to the alveolar gum ridge behind the front teeth:/t/ /d/ /n/ /l/ /s//z/

auditory: refers to hearing; information that one hears, pertaining to that part of the nervous system that processes information received through the ears

auditory discrimination: refers to determining fine differences between signals of information received through the ears or heard

auditory tracking: in this work refers to determining changes between the sequence of phonemes or discriminating changes in individual phonemes between syllables [i.e. crab vs. carb or pat vs. pit]

bade: old English word that is past tense for 'bid' as in "said good bye".

bide: wait, take your time

bilk: cheat someone of their money through trickery

bleat: sound made by a sheep

blem: a blemish

blend, blending: combine, tie together; in this work, combining sounds to figure out a word

bod: slang for 'body'

boon: a bonus, or blessing

bop: to hit, often on the head –"Little Bunny FooFoo hopping through the forest picking up the field mice and bopping them on the head" bot: piece of software that can execute commands

botch: to mess something up

bro: slang for 'brother'

ccvc: consonant-consonant-vowel-consonant

ccvcc: consonant-consonant-vowel-consonant-consonant

chock: from olden times when people used wagons. They put a wedge of wood against a wheel [called a chock] to keep it from moving.

cleat: a piece of metal shaped like a 'T' for wrapping rope around. Often found on a boat.

consonant: a sound or letter representing a sound that is formed by shaping or obstructing the air flow [any letter that is not a vowel]

cray: short for crayfish; or short for crazy

creed: a statement of belief

cud: partly digested food that a cow chews

cvc: consonant-vowel-consonant

cvcc: consonant-vowel-consonant-consonant

dap: style of fishing; let the fly bob touch the water, but do not let the line touch the water

decoding: assign sounds to letters in a pattern to figure out a written word

deleting: take away; in this work it refers to taking away a sound [i.e. Blake, bake, lake}

dell: a small valley as in "The Farmer in the Dell"

dental: sounds made in combination with the lips and teeth: /f/ /v/ /th/

dictate or dictation: tell someone what to write or the act of telling someone what to write

digraph: two letters that represent one sound - ph for /f/, ai for long vowel /a/, etc.

din: noise

Diphthong: a digraph or two letters for one vowel sound - as in /ea/ for the short e or long a sounds some diphthong vowel tones are neither long nor short. They are simply vowels [and that is all I tell the children before introducing the tones with possible ways of writing them] /oy/ /oi/ /ou/ /ow/ /oo/ /ir//er//ur/ /ar/ /or//air/ and /ear/. This work does not include lists for oy, oi, ou [ouch], ow [cow] diphthongs

encoding: to write letters, syllables in sequence to represent the sounds in words

flea: insect

flee: run away; Flee and flea are included here as an example of how the use of diphthongs helps the reader to understand word meanings.

floss: acronym for the doubling of consonants after a short vowel in a one syllable word -double f, l, and s after a short vowel

fram: name of a company that makes air filters for cars

fraught: full of something - usually has a negative connotation such as 'danger'

fray: threads separating or pulling away from the edge of cloth

gad: run around

isolate or isolation: separate something by itself; in this work separating a unit of sound from others in a syllable

labial: sounds made with the lips: /p/ /b/ /w/ /m/

lob: throw or toss

long vowels: sound like letter names.

lop: cut off

lull: a pause to sleep, relax, be quiet

mod: modern

mull: think something over

nib: pointed part of a pen where the ink comes out; a small piece of something like candy or corn

oral motor placement: using language to describe and associate the sound that is elicited to the placement and shaping of the tongue, teeth, lips and jaw

palatals: sounds produced when the tongue is raised toward the palate, or roof of the mouth: /y/ as in yes [requires a gliding movement of the jaw--the student may interpret two phonemes for this movement. Teach that it is a gliding movement having one letter]

palatao-alveolar: sounds elicited with the tongue high and close to the hard palate and pulled back slightly yet near the alveolar ridge: /r/ /sh/ /ch/ and /j/ as in judge/. The /zh/ sound, as in the word treasure, is also in this group; however, it is not included in the pages of this book.

pawn: a piece in a chess game

pesk: one who annoys or agitates

phoneme: an individual unit of sound within a syllable

phonemic processing: refers to the auditory system's ability to segment phonemes. People who are proficient in the area of phonemic processing are able to count the number of phonemes and say each sound in isolation.

phonological processing: refers to the ability to understand that sentences are comprised of separate words, process the space or break between words in an auditory signal, and the break between syllables in words. People proficient in the area phonological processing are able to count words in sentences and syllables in words; they are able to determine the ending of a sentence and the separation point between syllables.

pip: break through the shell of an egg; what a bird does when it hatches.

pith: spongy tissue in the center of a stem of a plant

plea: an appeal, a legal term for an appeal or attempt to defend

pod: the outside of a pea when it grows on a plant; compartment of a building

pog: a game played by flipping over small, flat cardboard disks

pro: short for professional

prone: likely to do something; or lying flat on the floor

rad: abbreviation for radius

reversal: change to opposite direction

rut: boring routine, long deep track usually made in the wet ground from tires

segmenting: separating

sequencing: in specific order

short vowels tones or phonemes produced in the front of the mouth from top [closed] to bottom [open] {short i, e, a, u, o}

slay: to kill

slew: to have a lot of something or past tense of slay

smidge: a little bit

spay: neuter a cat or dog

spew: to spit out

stake: wood or metal stick placed in the ground for a tent or fence

steak: cut of meat --- the words stake and steak are included to demonstrate how alternate spellings of words that sound the same helps the reader to understand word meanings.

syllable: unit of connected sounds within a word

tad: a little bit

tare: an old English word meaning 'weed'

tink: emit a high pitched noise such as a 'chirp'

tog: coat or cloak

tome: big, thick book

tot: small child

velar: sounds produced in the back of the mouth using the soft palate: /k/ /g/ /ng/

word family: a group of words that share a common base -i.e. might, fight, right; file, mile, pile

writ: a written command; word often used in legal documents

BIBLIOGRAPHY

Burns, Martha, Ph.D. "Auditory Processing Disorders, Dyslexia and Apraxia: Assessments and Evidence-BasedInterventions- Review of Neuroscience Applications and APD" https://www. northernspeech.com/language-communication-disorders/auditory-processing-disorders-dyslexia-and-apraxia-assessments-and-evidence-based-interventions/

Burns,Martha Ph.D. "Training Auditory Processing in Children with Autism Spectrum Disorders and other Developmental Disabilities,"https://www.northernspeech.com/uploads/images/e05/e05-Handout-PDF.pdf

Martha S. Burns, Ph.D. Director of Neuroscience Education Scientific Learning Corporation Adjunct Associate Professor Northwestern University February 28, 2015, "Update on Neuroscience Applications to Treating Speech, Language and Cognitive Disorders", http://www.scilearn.com/sites/default/files/pdf/presentations_vc/burns_-_feb_28th_morning_session_-_final_0.pdf

Sprenger-Charolles, Liliane, Colé, Pascale Fields, R Douglas "Change in Brain's White Matter" Science Vol 330, 5November2010

Turken, And U., Dronkers, Nina F. "The Neural Architecture of the Language Comprehension Network: Converging Evidence from Lesion and Connectivity Analyses" Frontiers in Systems Neuroscience published online February 10, 2011.

Masterson, Julie . Classroom Implementation of the Multilinguistic Model for Literacy Instruction, Missouri State University Literacy Lab http://nebula.wsimg.com/5cf5abb73bb a3ac04502e87b4af9909a?AccessKeyId=E197AE8D5240BD028530&disposition=0&allow origin=1

http://www.learningbydesign.com/research-and-results.htmlJeanne Wanzek, Brandy Gatlin, Stephanie Al Otaiba & Young-Suk Grace Kim "The Impact of Transcription Writing Interventions for First-Grade Students" Pages 1-16 | Published online: 20 Dec 2016 http://www. tandfonline.com/doi/full/10.1080/10573569.2016.1250142?scroll=top&needAccess=true

National Reading Panel (2000). Teaching children to read: An evidence-based assessment of the scientific research literature on reading and its implications for reading instruction [on-line]. Available: http://www.nichd.nih.gov/publications/nrp/smallbook.htm.

National Research Council (1998). <u>Preventing reading difficulties in young children</u>. Washington, DC: National Academy Press.

Kenn Apel*,1, Julie J. Masterson2 "Comparing the Spelling and Reading Abilities of Students With Cochlear Implants and Students With Typical Hearing"; <u>Journal of Deaf Studies and Deaf Education</u>, 2015, 125–135; doi:10.1093/deafed/env002 Advance Access publication February 17, 2015 Empirical Manuscript

<u>Kenn Apel</u> and <u>Julie J. Masterson</u> featured Language Speech and Hearing Services in the Schools July 2001, Vol. 32, 182-195. doi:10.1044/0161-1461(2001/017)

Robertson,Carolyn, M.Ed. and Salter, Wanda, MS. CCC-SLP. Phonological Awareness Test 2 (PAT 2) available at http://www4.parinc.com or www.Linguisystems.com

Printed in the United States
By Bookmasters